T0365724

Cambridge Elements ☰

Elements in Theatre, Performance and the Political
edited by
Trish Reid
University of Reading
Liz Tomlin
University of Glasgow

STAGING CLASS CONFLICT
IN THE UK

Liz Tomlin
University of Glasgow

CAMBRIDGE
UNIVERSITY PRESS

Shaftesbury Road, Cambridge CB2 8EA, United Kingdom

One Liberty Plaza, 20th Floor, New York, NY 10006, USA

477 Williamstown Road, Port Melbourne, VIC 3207, Australia

314–321, 3rd Floor, Plot 3, Splendor Forum, Jasola District Centre,
New Delhi – 110025, India

103 Penang Road, #05–06/07, Visioncrest Commercial, Singapore 238467

Cambridge University Press is part of Cambridge University Press & Assessment,
a department of the University of Cambridge.

We share the University's mission to contribute to society through the pursuit
of education, learning and research at the highest international levels of excellence.

www.cambridge.org
Information on this title: www.cambridge.org/9781009598613

DOI: 10.1017/9781009394222

First published 2025

A catalogue record for this publication is available from the British Library

ISBN 978-1-009-59861-3 Hardback
ISBN 978-1-009-39424-6 Paperback
ISSN 2753-1244 (online)
ISSN 2753-1236 (print)

Cambridge University Press & Assessment has no responsibility for the persistence
or accuracy of URLs for external or third-party internet websites referred to in this
publication and does not guarantee that any content on such websites is, or will
remain, accurate or appropriate.

Staging Class Conflict in the UK

Elements in Theatre, Performance and the Political

DOI: 10.1017/9781009394222
First published online: March 2025

Liz Tomlin
University of Glasgow
Author for correspondence: Liz Tomlin, Elizabeth.Tomlin@glasgow.ac.uk

Abstract: This Element focuses on the frequent staging of the most precarious fraction of the working class in the context of a theatre industry, academy and audiences that are dominated by the cultural fraction of the middle class. It interrogates the staging of an abjectified figure as a means of challenging the stigmatisation of the poor in political discourse, defined here as an ideological imaginary of moral and cultural deficit. The Element argues that in seeking to subvert such an imaginary, theatre that stages the abjectified subject may risk consolidating two further imaginaries of working-class deficit that have been confected in political discourse from the 1990s to the 2020s. In conclusion, the Element reflects on the political potential of theatre that rather seeks to eradicate class descriptors, conflicts and hierarchies altogether. This title is also available as Open Access on Cambridge Core.

Keywords: theatre, precarious, political, working class, cultural industries

ISBNs: 9781009598613 (HB), 9781009394246 (PB), 9781009394222 (OC)
ISSNs: 2753-1244 (online), 2753-1236 (print)

Contents

1 Introduction

This Element is one of the principle outcomes of my AHRC fellowship (2022–24), *Figurations of working class subjects in UK theatre practice and policy*.[1] Over a period of eighteen months I engaged in dialogues with theatre scholars, sociologists, artists, producers and policy makers, identifying the multiple class inequities that persist throughout the theatre industry in the UK today. For this Element, I wanted to dig more deeply into the ideological implications of certain patterns that emerged throughout the research: the dominance within the theatre industry and audiences of those from a particular section of the middle class; the common recurrence of staged figures of precarity; the placement of this figure in antagonistic relationship to, or allyship with, the audience; and the popularity of autobiographical accounts of lived experiences of precarity. In my conversations with sociologists, I also became increasingly aware that defining class itself has never been more complex.

1.1 Classification

There are many different approaches to class in current sociological thinking. These include use of the existing NS-SEC socio-economic classifications;[2] development of new socio-economic schema to reflect changing trends in employment (Savage *et al.*, 2015); and analysis that continues to emphasise the importance of cultural and social, as well as economic, capital, as introduced by sociologist Pierre Bourdieu (2010). In addition, the intersections of race, gender, geography and age, among other factors, can no longer be ignored. Demographic research into social mobility, or the lack of it, also requires a distinction between class origin (most often assessed by the class of job done by the main breadwinner of your family when you were aged fourteen[3]) and class destination (the classification of the job that you currently do).

No definitions, including those drawn on in this Element, are authoritative, although some are more evidence-based than others. All are strategic, contestable, imperfect and incomplete categorisations of human subjects within which innumerable exceptions will always exist. Moreover, the very act of classification is not a neutral, or merely descriptive, one. As Imogen Tyler cautions, all

---

[1] AH/W005999/1; University of Glasgow – Subjects A-Z – Theatre Studies – Research – Figurations of working class subjects in UK theatre practice and policy.

[2] Established by John Goldthorpe in the 1970s and still used today by the Office of National Statistics The National Statistics Socio-economic classification (NS-SEC) – Office for National Statistics (ons.gov.uk).

[3] This is the question recently adopted by Arts Council England surveys to map how many working-class-origin artists/creatives were employed by the arts organisations they funded. Equality, Diversity and Inclusion: A Data Report, 2020–2021 | Arts Council England.

classificatory systems play a part in creating and legitimating 'the forms of value, judgements and norms they establish in human societies' (2015: 507). This is where theatre and performance can productively intervene, as this Element will explore, by staging the fictions of classed identities precisely in order to expose their ideological slipperiness and subvert the normative values that classificatory systems can consolidate. Nonetheless, however double-edged, subjective and provisional sociological classifications are, they are tools that are sometimes necessary to address the reality of contemporary Britain, a country that is, and always has been, riven by class inequality, however that is precisely defined, understood, or even experienced.[4] The easier-to-evidence material inequality of economic resources, educational opportunity, health chances and life choices is also driven by class stigmatisation and cultural and social practices of privilege and exclusion which are less easy to quantify but no less real. Without ways of identifying and naming those who benefit most from such inequality, and those who pay the biggest cost, political operations of redress or reparation cannot be designed or undertaken.

Since around 2015, there has been an acceleration, in theatre and perform-ance studies, of interest in class inequality, which this Element will draw on, develop and interrogate. One significant departure from existing studies is my commitment to employing class fractions: more precise classifications than the categories of middle and working class commonly encountered in theatre scholarship. Such precision is not only valuable in its own right but also productively complicates the often assumed inter-class antagonism between these two broad class constructs that might rather conceal, as this Element will demonstrate, other nuanced and pluralistic inter-class allyships and intra-class conflicts that are critical to examine. The class protagonists central to this study are, firstly, the *cultural fraction* of the middle class that, as I will evidence in Section 2, make up the majority of artists, audiences and academics who are the taste-makers and architects of the cultural field of consumption and, secondly, the most *precarious fraction* of the working class which has become an increas-ingly common figure of political concern on the stages of British theatre.

The descriptor of the 'cultural fraction' draws on Bourdieu's historical division of the middle class into two fractions 'defined by different asset structures, i.e., different distributions of their total capital among the different kinds of capital' (2010:109). On the one hand is the fraction that is high in economic capital, but less endowed with cultural capital. Bourdieu includes, 'industrial and commercial employers at the higher level, craftsmen and

---

4 See, for example, Bottero (2004) for a discussion of resistance to self-classification, and Beswick (2020) for a discussion of the importance of class identity as affectively felt and experienced.

shopkeepers at the intermediate level' (109). On the other is the fraction that concerns us here, those who hold relatively less economic capital but higher levels of cultural capital. This cultural fraction, despite variations in income, would incorporate most of those working in the cultural and creative industries, given the necessity for a degree in most jobs in this sector and the high levels of cultural capital held. The cultural fraction would also encompass the majority of those working at primary, secondary and higher levels of education as highlighted by Bourdieu (109), as well as other comparable graduate professions.

Increasingly staged as antagonist to the cultural fraction of the middle class anticipated to make up the most part of the audience is the figure of the precarious subject, drawn from the most disenfranchised fraction of the working class. It is the complex relationship between these two class fractions that is the central concern of this Element. Given the different uses, in political and philosophical theory, to which the term 'precarious' has been put (Standing, 2011; Butler, 2015: 15), it is important to note that my use of it here is drawing on a recent classification scheme devised by sociologist Mike Savage. The precariat fraction is the lowest of Savage *et al.*'s seven classifications and comprises the unemployed and the most precarious zero-hours workers (2015).[5] In John Goldthorpe's NS-SEC scheme, the precariat would align to the ninth and lowest category of 'never worked and long term unemployed'.[6]

1.2 Setting the Stage

The subsidised professional sector of the theatre industry is the setting in which the relationship between these two protagonists will be explored.[7] This sector is consecrated within the academy as the one in which aesthetic and cultural value is most highly regarded, given that it dominates the stages of the flagship national venues and regional theatres, and most often represents the nations of the UK on international festival and touring circuits. Unlike most sporting events, musicals or popular music, it is funded, or part-funded, by the state

---

[5] This consisted of seven classifications: 1. Elite; 2. Established middle class; 3. Technical middle class; 4. New affluent workers; 5. Traditional working class; 6. Emerging service workers; 7. Precariat (Savage *et al.* 2015: 174).

[6] This consists of nine classifications that do not include full-time students: 1.1 Large employers and higher managerial and administrative occupations; 1.2 Higher professional occupations; 2. Lower managerial, administrative and professional occupations; 3. Intermediate occupations; 4. Small employers and own account workers; 5. Lower supervisory and technical occupations; 6. Semi-routine occupations; 7. Routine occupations; 8. Never worked and long-term unemployed (Savage *et al.*, 2015: 41).

[7] Theatre activity subsidised by the arts councils that is directed towards the staging of non-professional performers makes a brief appearance in the final section of this study, but would require an Element of its own to fully interrogate the particular class dynamics operating in those contexts.

because it is implicitly assigned a cultural value for the nation that places it beyond 'mere' entertainment and, consequently, is assumed to be unable to attract sufficient mass-appeal to rely on solely commercial models of funding.

As I will evidence in Section 2, increased sociological analysis of all cultural and creative industries, as well as theatre and performance in particular, has produced research that conclusively establishes the dominance of these sectors (including, for the most part, their audiences) by those of middle-class origin, despite their public funding base comprising a combination of taxation and lottery proceeds drawn from the much wider population. The subsidised professional theatre sector is thus distinguished by class inequality, cultural currency and limited popular appeal.[8] Indeed, as Bourdieu notes, in order to hold cultural capital, limited popular appeal is essential, as it constitutes, for those who do participate, the mark of distinction and evidence of a cultural taste that is more refined than mass cultural activity (2010: 23). This necessity for, and acknowledgement of, cultural distinction makes the subsidised professional theatre sector a fascinating case study for class analysis as it establishes the very conception of the sector itself as a playground of high cultural capital consecrated, firstly, by state funding via the national arts councils and, secondly, by theatre academics who predominantly select from this field to establish curricula in university departments that confirm, for the artists and cultural leaders of the future, how and where cultural capital is held.

The stage that is set for the exploration of class conflicts in this Element extends beyond the plays and autobiographical performances that will be the key focus of this study. Rather, it encompasses various and complex classed configurations and antagonistic relationships of artists, audiences, those who are imagined to be absent or excluded from the theatre and those who make up the cultural and creative leadership of the theatre industry and related scholarly disciplines. Moreover, the analysis of performances will be undertaken in the context of class conflicts, both rhetorical and real, that are staged in the wider social and political conditions of the time. This contextualisation affords an ideological analysis of the conditions underpinning the aesthetic choices made, and reveals the possible political consequences of those choices on perceptions of class allegiances and antagonisms in the wider cultural and political field. Such consequences, of course, lead us full circle as they contribute, in turn, to the ideological conditions of production determining which future performances are most likely to be supported and made.

---

[8] See Brook, O'Brien and Taylor (2020) for figures on cultural attendance in England: 'attendance at most art and cultural forms is a minority activity. Film was the major outlier' (94–95).

1.3 Political Context

Section 2, **Class Antagonisms and Alliances on the Political Stage**, will set out the political context that provides the ideological backdrop for the performance analysis in the sections that follow. It will begin by fleshing out the figure of the cultural fraction of the middle class and introducing the creative subset of this fraction that comprises the theatre makers and academics who produce and analyse the work under examination in this Element. It will then highlight the alliance between the creative subset of this class fraction and the frequently staged figure drawn from the most precarious fraction of the working class. Given that this alliance grows out of an ideological imperative to challenge the stigmatisation of such a figure on the political stage, I will then chart the first of two political operations that are central to this study: the Labour Government's (1997–2010) cleavage of the working class into 'hard-working families' versus an unemployed underclass who were increasingly stigmatised as figures of abjection in poverty porn documentaries such as Channel Four's *Benefits Street* (2014), or satirical comedy such as BBC's *Little Britain* (2003–2006).

This stigmatisation, examined at length by Imogen Tyler, positions the poorest subjects in society as the abject 'waste' of increasingly cruel 'neoliberal economic, political and social policies' (2013: 8). Historically, as Beverley Skeggs argues, the poor have always been seen less as unfortunate victims of an unfair economic system than essentialised as biologically degenerate and inferior human beings who are closer to animals and children than adult human subjects who have accrued the necessary cultural and moral values (Skeggs, 2004: 37). Furthermore, Skeggs critiques Bourdieu's own portrayal of the working class noting that 'these subjects appear with negative capital, as lack, deficit, a void of value' (Skeggs, 2011: 502). Such stigmatisation is thus defined in this study as an *ideological imaginary* of deficit, and it is this ideological imaginary that the theatre-makers featured here seek to challenge through their staging of protagonists drawn from this class fraction.

The second political operation to be examined in Section 2 is that of a right-wing populism which has sought to divide the working class into those who 'belong' here (implicitly those who are white) and those who are 'foreign outsiders' (explicitly asylum seekers). In this rhetorical narrative, white working- and lower-middle-class fractions are hailed as 'ordinary people' and placed in antagonistic relations, not only with those classed as outsiders but also with the well-known populist antagonist, the 'elite', a rhetorical figure into which the cultural fraction of the middle class squarely falls. The danger for theatre makers and academics is the risk of accepting this confected conflict, and with it the populist narrative, in which those framed as their antagonists are assumed to hold the views that are attributed to them via the strategic and rhetorical figure of 'ordinary people'. This, I argue, conjures up a re-directed ideological imaginary of moral deficit in which the figure of the white working- or lower-middle-class subject is no longer conflated with a figure of abjection, but of racist recidivism.

1.4 Three Ideological Imaginaries of Deficit

The remaining sections of this Element will examine three different manifestations of the ideological imaginary of deficit through the analysis of selected plays and performances. The political imperative, of theatre makers and scholars, to challenge the stigmatisation of the most precarious fraction of the working class underpins much of the work explored in this Element and will be the focus of my analysis in Section 3, **Staging the Ideological Imaginary of Deficit**, through examinations of Gary Owen's *Iphigenia in Splott* (2015), Kieran Hurley's *Mouthpiece* (2018) and Chris Bush's *Hungry* (2021). In each of these plays the audience is interpellated as complicit in the internalisation of the ideological imaginary of deficit and so in need of provocation, but I will suggest that this may not always be the case. The cultural fraction of the middle class that makes up the most part of such audiences has always been, as Bourdieu proposes, and I will further discuss, distinguished by its left-wing political leanings (2010: 439). Thus, the majority of spectators are likely to self-identify as the political ally of the precarious figures staged, which can result in the evocation of new manifestations of the ideological imaginary of deficit, as the subsequent two sections will explore.

In Section 4, **Artists and Agency**, I examine, through Arinzé Kene's autofictional[9] performance, *Misty* (2018), and Scottee's autobiographical performance, *Class* (2019), how one new manifestation of the ideological imaginary comes into play when the figures of precarity being staged, or narrated, are real people, or ostensibly so. Extending the self-reflective interrogation threaded through both pieces, and drawing on Katie Beswick's (2019) work on authenticity, I argue that the ideological imperative for the cultural fraction of the middle class to ally with the figure of precarity is precisely what raises the risk of exoticisation. Narratives of authentic precarity become required by such audiences to afford them the pleasure of offering the allyship that confirms and consolidates both their own distance from precarity (in most cases) and their distinctive political identity within the cultural, rather than economic, fraction of the middle class.

Given the risks of exoticisation, which both Scottee and Kene acknowledge, it is inevitable that the working-class-origin artists contracted to provide such

---

[9] See Mark, 2024, for the first significant study of autofictional performance.

accounts are, themselves, implicitly reduced to figures of cultural deficit, valued not for their craft or creative capacity, but only for the authenticity of their lived experience of precarity. Thus, regardless of the cultural agency they appear to be afforded by their place at the heart of the creative subset of the cultural fraction, there is a risk that the industry expectations that, often unconsciously, shape their origin narratives ghost a second manifestation of the figure of cultural deficit which, I propose, echoes Jacques Rancière's (2003) figure of the shoe-maker that successive philosophers have fought to keep out of the intellectual arena. Moreover, if the artist's authenticated lived experience of precarity is presented, not as exceptional, nor as that pertaining to a particular fraction, but rather as a stand-in for that of the working class more broadly, there is a danger that precarity and at times its abjectification become synonymous with the working-class subject per se, thus reconfirming a middle-class imaginary of an always precarious, sometimes abjectified, working class.

In Section 5, **Allyship and Antagonism**, I will deconstruct the significant body of scholarly analysis of Jez Butterworth's *Jerusalem* (2009) to suggest that the lens through which the play has commonly been assessed is a classed lens that conceals how the allyship between the abjectified outsider and the cultural fraction of the middle class can be employed to vilify and demonise the life-choices and ethical perspectives of those who, in the play, are located as antagonists to the alliance of Rooster and the interpellated audience. These are the residents of the new estate who, while ambiguously classed by Butterworth, and variously classed by theatre scholars, are most persuasively understood as aspirational working or lower middle class or, in Dan Evans' (2023) terms, the traditional fraction of the petty-bourgeoisie. This section will suggest that the nature of the classed representations in *Jerusalem* and the alliances and antagonisms invited highlight the dangers of an uncritical absorp-tion of the antagonism confected by the far right between the cultural fraction of the middle class and the white working- and lower-middle-class fractions. The result is an evocation of a new imaginary of cultural and moral deficit in which the white working- or lower-middle-class figure becomes synonymous with bad taste, complicity with neoliberal consumerism, and racist violence.

1.5 The Political Potential of Declassification

In Section 6, **Making Theatre by Making Shoes (and Other Things) Together**, I will depart from performances that stage class conflict to examine whether *12 Last Songs* (2021) by Quarantine Theatre might offer different answers to the questions that this Element has posed. Might an avoidance of explicit class conflict, in favour of work which purposefully declassifies and equalises subjects from across the classes, offer an alternative mode of resistance to the ideological imaginary of deficit which relies on classification and distinction between the classes for its power? Here, I continue to think with Jacques Rancière, whose philosophy has been seminal in arguing against classification more broadly, and that of the working-class subject in particular.

Ultimately, I suggest, alternatives are important because there are risks to the political operation of de-stigmatising the figuration of abjection, as highlighted above in 1.4, that need to be brought more sharply into focus. The interest of theatre makers and academics in the most precarious fraction of the working class is understandable and necessary, given the demonisation of such a fraction in political discourse. However, a focus on this fraction at the expense of broader fractions of the working and lower middle classes will ensure that the latter (who are minoritised in the theatre sector, subsidised theatre audiences and arts academia) remain occluded from the debate. Their concerns and critical perspectives will not be permitted to challenge the ideological convictions of the dominant class fraction, their representations will remain rare, and the classist barricades within which the cultural sector operates (Brook *et al.,* 2020; Tomlin *et al.*, 2020) will be further strengthened to resist any dilution of the political or cultural consensus that has evolved.

This Element hopes, beyond the analysis featured here, to encourage its readers to seek out their own arguments to challenge and interrogate the ideological coherence of the sector. If we begin to pay close attention to the classed lens of our discipline, and the theatre industry itself, we might, as scholars, teachers, artists or students, start to expose existing classed hierarchies and make space for, and valorise, a greater diversity of classed perspectives and interventions. In this way, we will all be better placed to challenge and overturn the antagonisms that political rhetoric, on both the right and the left, has evoked, as the following section will now explore.

2 Class Antagonisms and Alliances on the Political Stage

2.1 The Cultural Fraction of the Middle Class

It is of little surprise that audiences of subsidised theatre are chiefly comprised of individuals from the cultural fraction of the middle class. In *Culture Is Bad for You*, Orian Brook, Dave O'Brien and Mark Taylor evidence that audiences for drama are dominated by the professional and managerial class, outnumbering those in routine or semi-routine occupations by around 3:1 (2020: 84). Brook *et al.* also confirm the predominance, within 'formal' cultural attendance (which would include subsidised theatre), of the 'higher *professional*' rather than the 'higher *managerial*' class fraction of the middle class (97 my emphasis). This is unsurprising given that the higher professional fraction comprised of university lecturers, doctors and lawyers corresponds closely with Bourdieu's cultural fraction. Furthermore, Brook *et al.* demonstrate that 'Artistic and literary occupations have a particularly distinctive pattern of [cultural] engagement. They are the most engaged in the formal cultural activities that ... are of interest to the smallest minority of the population' (98).

This sub-fraction of 'artistic and literary occupations' offers a more precise understanding of those who play a key role in this Element: the artists and producers who create the theatre and those working in related academic disciplines, often themselves former artists, who analyse and valorise it. These all belong to, what might be understood as, an 'uber-cultural' creative subsection of Bourdieu's fraction, or a 'micro class' (Brook *et al.,* 2020: 18) within the cultural fraction of the middle class more broadly. Moreover, there is ample evidence that those working within the cultural and creative industries are overwhelmingly of middle-class origin (Brook *et al.,* 2020: 63). The middle-class-origin dominance of creative occupations more broadly is repeated, if not accentuated, in research that extrapolates data on theatre in particular. In the 2016 *Analysis of Theatre in England* report, concern was expressed that 'social mobility in the sector is not increasing; rather, it may be regressing'.[10] In their study of the 'class ceiling' in the acting profession, Friedman *et al.* report that '73 per cent of actors in the GBCS [Great British Class Survey] ... come from "middle class" professional or managerial backgrounds whereas this group constitutes only 29 per cent of the population ... Moreover, only 10 per cent of actors in the GBCS ... have parents who worked in semi-routine and routine employment, or who never worked, compared with 33 per cent' of a representative data set (Friedman, O'Brien and Laurison, 2017: 997). In *The Director's Voice*, the authors reported that 79 per cent of the workforce was made up of directors 'who come from what is categorised as either an upper-middle class or middle class background', in contrast with only 27 per cent of the population as a whole (Hescott and Furness, 2018: 22).

This cumulative research and advocacy has gained traction in policy terms, in England in particular. Not only has Arts Council England's funding emphasis shifted towards a significant redistribution of funding in favour of areas previously under-resourced by cultural subsidy,[11] but it has also now included socio-economic diversity in the cultural workforce surveys of national portfolio organisations, to sit alongside the existing protected characteristics of race, gender and disability.[12] However, in his article, 'Class and the problem of inequality in the theatre', Dave O'Brien ultimately concludes that neither

---

[10] https://www.artscouncil.org.uk/publication/theatreinengland
[11] Let's Create | Arts Council England.
[12] Equality, Diversity and Inclusion: A Data Report, 2020–2021 | Arts Council England.

raising the visibility of class nor even acting on it to improve the demographics of class composition in the theatre industry will be sufficient to shift class discrimination which 'is bound up with struggles over cultural expressions and what counts as legitimate' (2020: 247).

This is because the predominance of those of middle-class origin within the creative subset that comprises the cultural industries and related academic disciplines not merely is a demographic imbalance but also ensures that the behavioural norms, aesthetic values and ideological convictions of this subset wield near-hegemonic authority within the industry and academy – both what is produced in the first place and, subsequently, what is consecrated as holding high cultural value through academic syllabi and publications. Brook *et al.* do not claim that these ideological convictions are monolithic, and they are keen to distinguish their micro-class from the 'creative class' of economic and policy analyst, Richard Florida (2002). Nonetheless, their research demonstrates that '[i]n Britain's cultural occupations we can see a coherent set of values and attitudes that are liberal, left-wing, and in favour of welfare and security interventions ... of all the industrial groups measured, people working in cultural and creative industries have the most left-wing, liberal, pro-welfare values' (2020: 67). This is not, of course, to suggest that differently classed subjects, or workers in other industrial classifications, do not share such values, or to deny that there may be some individuals among the micro-class of creative workers who do not. The significant claim here is that in no other industrial group measured was there found to be so much ideological coherence among its workers. The dominance of a single class origin, within this particular industrial grouping, exacerbates the risk of a classed hegemony of shared norms and aesthetics which must then be protected from challenge, propagated and sustained. So long as the prevailing cultural legitimation of certain aesthetics, representations and ideological assumptions remains undisturbed, individual artists of whatever class origin will always be required to assimilate into the existing habitus, in order to succeed within it.

2.2 Allyship with the Precarious Fraction of the Working Class

The conclusions of Brook *et al.* suggest that the left-wing political values shared by a significant majority of the creative subset, including theatre artists, would inevitably evoke empathy for the most precarious fraction of the working class. The political intention of staging figures from this particular class fraction is most commonly undertaken, as demonstrated in the plays examined here, to challenge mainstream stigmatisation of those who, as this section will go on to examine, are economically marginalised under the mechanisms of neoliberalism and have been culturally denigrated and abjectified in political discourse and the narratives of a hostile and influential right-wing media. The academic interest in plays addressing the plight of the marginalised would suggest that theatre scholars in the UK, for the most part, hold similar political convictions to the creative subset of artists. The evidence of any examination of scholarly publications shows a sector that has always leaned strongly to the left,[13] but there has recently been a particular interest in theatre that deals explicitly with, and offers allyship to, the most economically disenfranchised subjects, as can be seen from signifi- cant British publications during the period in question (e.g. Jeffers, 2012; Angelaki, 2017; Fragkou, 2018; Beswick, 2019; Holdsworth, 2020; Bartley, 2020).

Class origin, of individual artist or academic, can also, of course, explain this allyship, if distinct from the class destination of the creative subset entered into, but the solidarity shown by the creative and scholarly output of the subset as a whole is ample evidence of the ideological allyship that exists, regardless of the particular class origin of those directly concerned. The broadly shared political operation behind the theatre under analysis in the publications noted (among many more) is an analysis of the consequences of neoliberal economics on the poorest fraction of the working-class, however defined, and a subversion of the stigmatising ideological imaginary of deficit as detailed in the introduction.

However, there are hidden dangers in such allyship, especially when the political operation of the play is intended to subvert the ideological imaginary of deficit by first setting up a figure who appears to exemplify precisely the tropes of abjection of such an imaginary. These dangers are, indeed, highlighted in many of the existing publications identified above, most notably in those of Beswick and Holdsworth, and will be further developed in Section 3 in my analysis of *Mouthpiece* and *Iphigenia in Splott*. Given that the majority of those in the theatre audiences in question will not share a class background with such protagonists, there is a real danger that the identifications utilised in the theatre productions to 'mark' the protagonists as subjects of precarity risk perpetuating the all-too-familiar tropes of abjection that have come to both define and capture 'the poor' as understood by spectators whose only knowledge of those living such lives is via the poverty porn lens of a hostile right-wing media.

In her analysis of social abjection in English theatre, Nadine Holdsworth remarks on the cultural appetite for theatre featuring such subjects (2020: 52),

---

[13] The preponderance of analysis of left-wing theatres and practices would be too extensive to list. It is significant to point to one rare exception, *Vanguard Performance Beyond Left and Right*, (Jannarone, 2015), that explicitly seeks to address this disciplinary lacuna in identifying how the avant-garde has also operated on the right, and far right, of the political spectrum.

and proposes that such 'theatre invites relational encounters so that the figure cast as socially abject might be made visible, regarded and understood anew' (15). But she also warns of the danger that theatre-makers might 'be drawn to recirculating these images in a way that becomes a self-perpetuating discursive practice' (52). As well as the dangers of abjectification, examined here in Sections 3 and 4, there is a risk that if the precarious subject is the most recurrent and hyper-visible example of working-class figuration seen on our stages, it might become, by default, the stand-in for the working class more broadly, thus reducing the working-class subject to a figure of precarity only, in the ideo-logical imaginary of the predominantly middle-class audience. As I will now detail, this risks reflecting the erasure of the working class as it is cleaved into middle class on the one hand and underclass on the other, in the political operations of the social stage over recent decades.

2.3 The Erasure of the Working Class

This argument was proposed by political commentator Owen Jones, who argued that the most critical consequence of the '"chavs" phenomenon' was the 'attempt to obscure the reality of the working class majority' (2016: 6). Challenging the myth that located '[n]ice, middle class people on one side' and 'an unredeemable detritus on the other' (7), Jones pertinently asked, 'Where the millions who remain in manual occupations ... fit into all this is an interesting question' (7). As Jones (2016) and Imogen Tyler (2013) both argue, the reduction of the diversity of the working class to the singular and stigmatised figure of the 'chav' was initiated in the 1980s and consolidated throughout the 1990s and 2000s (Tyler, 2013: 163–171).

Under Conservative prime minister Margaret Thatcher (1979–1990) the industrial working class had been literally decimated through the closure of mines, shipyards, steelworks and other heavy industries that had historically constituted the main part of working-class labour and identity. This was fol-lowed, Tyler argues, in the New Labour years (1997–2010) by a discursive fragmentation of the historical 'working class subject' that resulted from Prime Minister Tony Blair's insistence on meritocracy and welfare reform (2013: 158–163). As Tyler argues, 'the discourses of meritocracy and choice that saturated public culture and policy documents functioned as an alibi for economic inequalities' (162). This enabled poverty to be located not as a material consequence of structural inequality but as a lifestyle choice of those who lacked the aspiration or capacity to transcend it. As Tyler concludes, 'within the space of a decade the idea that it was a poverty of aspiration, the failure to make the "right choices" and an unwillingness to grasp the opportunities gifted by the state which were to blame for intergenerational cultures of worklessness was established as a powerful myth' (161).

This drew a dividing line through communities who had previously understood themselves as working class, fracturing them into, as Tyler concludes, either 'hard-working families',[14] who were on the meritocratic, social mobility ladder, or the derogatory figure of the work-shy 'chav'. Through this fragmentation, the very idea of the working-class subject was ultimately dispensed with, as Satnam Virdee and Brendan McGeever confirm (2023: 102). Phrases such as 'hard-working families' embodied Labour's promise to reward an 'aspirational' working class (103) no longer explicitly identified in classed terms, while simultaneously pathologising the unemployed who had failed to become productive neoliberal subjects. The unemployed were abjected from classification (now an 'underclass') and portrayed as the failures of a meritocratic society in which they had been given every chance to succeed, and the 'hard-working families' were encouraged to believe that they were 'all middle class now' – or that was, at the very least, the desired destination.[15] At the same time, the actual middle class, as defined by the official statistics, was indeed growing rapidly (Evans and Tilley, 2017: 6–7), thus compounding the symbolic erasure of the working class with an actual reduction in their demographic share and political significance.

Despite the demographic shift described by Evans and Tilley, the rhetorical phrase 'hard-working families' was, as Virdee and McGeever argue, 'far from an innocent response to empirical changes in the class structure, [. . . but rather] a concerted attempt to remake class itself' (2023: 102). Virdee and McGeever's analysis highlights the importance of class to those hailed as 'hard working families', but the avoidance of any explicit class component enables the rhetorical figure to shape-shift as required.[16] When addressed to the aspirational working class Virdee and McGeever describe, the figure should importantly be understood to also encompass, as Dan Evans argues (2023: 79), the 'traditional

---

[14] For more on 'hard-working families' see Wheeler, 2005; Todd, 2014; and Runswick-Cole, Lawthom and Goodley, 2016.

[15] In the run-up to the 1997 General Election, John Prescott (to become the deputy leader of the incoming Labour Government) was regularly cited in the press as claiming 'we are all middle class now', although that has since been denied. The sentiment, however, of this New Labour vision for the country is repeated throughout many of the speeches of Prime Minister Tony Blair. Perhaps most notably his speech to the Institute for Public Policy Research (14 January 1999), where he promised 'A middle class which will include millions of people who may traditionally see themselves as working class'. BBC News | UK Politics | Blair promises decade of power.

[16] The phrase is used in the *Daily Telegraph*, for example, for workers earning upwards of £40,000 a year in articles concerned with higher-rate taxes. See Telegraph Readers, 2020; Brennan, 2021; Denham, 2024.

petty bourgeoisie', a lower middle-class fraction – often of working-class origin – that would comprise, in the Goldthorpe scheme, small employers and own account workers: for example, shopkeepers, tradespeople, skilled manual labourers and craftspeople.

The antagonistic figuration of the 'underclass' of the non-working poor, on the other side of the binary, was, as Tyler (2013) recounts, one of abject waste – both in the sense of being blamed as unproductive neoliberal subjects who leeched off the work of others and in the sense of being shamed for their moral and cultural failure to live their lives according to middle-class norms. This 'weaponisation of stigma' (Scambler, 2018)[17] was significantly sharpened in the decade of austerity (2010–2019) to insistently set 'shirkers' against 'strivers'.[18] This repeated rhetoric of Prime Minister David Cameron's Tory-led administration (2010–2015) was intended to build public support for brutal cuts to welfare, and to encourage the 'working' working- and lower-middle-class subjects, now collated and interpellated as 'hard-working families', to direct their sense of injustice for the austerity-imposed hardships towards the 'underclass' (which included asylum seekers prevented from employment) who were perceived as taking advantage, and an unfair share, of the shrinking state resources that were available.

Given this recent history of the abjectification of the non-working poor, it is unsurprising that the political values held by the most part of the subsidised theatre sector, and theatre academics, have led to the regular staging of the most precarious subjects in order to challenge and overturn the weaponisation of stigma on the political stage, as I will discuss in Section 3, **Staging the Ideological Imaginary of Deficit**. Nonetheless, the repetition of this figure on the theatre stage does compound the relative absence from subsidised theatre of the wider working-class fractions which are less often staged, and just as minoritised in theatre audiences as the precarious fraction themselves. The dominance of the cultural fraction of the middle class in the audiences of subsidised theatre, and the preference for figures of precarity on its stages, thus repeats, in the auditorium, the erasure of the working class more broadly that Owen and Tyler have documented.

The emphasis can also, as I'll discuss in Section 4, **Artists and Agency**, risk reducing the very idea of the working-class subject to one of precarity, if not abjection, and sustain an imaginary of cultural deficit that continues to stick to working-class-origin artists. These unintended side-effects of the political operation to subvert the ideological imaginary of the most precarious fraction suggest a need, within the creative subset of theatre makers and academics, to

---

[17] See also Tyler and Slater, 2018.
[18] This phrase featured in a Conservative ad. Campaign in 2012.

engage with a broader representation of working-class fractions, in order to bring them – both figuratively and literally – into a cultural space in which their diverse lived experiences and perspectives are valued. This need becomes increasingly vital in light of the second political operation of interest here, and the confected antagonism I will now turn to: that between so-called 'ordinary people' and those branded 'the cultural elite'.

2.4 Confecting Antagonism towards 'the Cultural Elite'

The antagonistic bifurcation of the old working class into aspirant versus abjectified was not the only lasting outcome of New Labour's policies to eradicate the historical idea of working-class solidarity. Virdee and McGeever describe how the refusal of New Labour to revive the socialist language of class, in the wake of Thatcher's decimation of working-class industries and communities, resulted in a carve up of

> the defeated working class into different ethno-racialized appellations: on the one hand there was the white working class, now racialised as white and associated with the decline and deviance of the council estate. Meanwhile Britons of Caribbean and Asian descent were presented as classless, racialized subjects to be celebrated as multicultural British success stories or denigrated, in the case of Muslims, as 'unassimilable'. (106)

Virdee and McGeever go on to add to this list the demonisation of asylum seekers, the Roma community and young black men whose culture was held to blame for the rise in knife and gun crime (106–108). This 'racialized politics of class' (117), a direct result of New Labour's erasure of socialist class politics, weakened the potential for multi-ethnic working-class solidarity and was, as I will now detail, to lay fertile ground from which a classed and raced antagonism could be confected and harnessed in the hard-right's forthcoming pursuit of Brexit and beyond.

When the figure of the working-class subject finally made its return to mainstream discourse in the 2016 campaign to leave the European Union (and subsequently in Boris Johnson's 2019 electoral campaign and victory that followed), it was to be clothed in a number of rhetorical disguises that never spoke explicitly of class, enabling it to be as shape-shifting as the political uses it was put to. In the battle for Brexit, it re-appeared in the rhetorical figure of the 'left-behind' that, unlike the cleavage under previous administrations described above in 2.3, encompassed both working and non-working subjects from (usually post-industrial) working-class communities. However, the figure of the 'left-behind' was to be regularly employed to fracture the working class in even more dangerous ways. In the Brexit campaign, this figure was harnessed by anti-immigration rhetoric, exemplified by hostility towards Eastern European workers and Nigel Farage's infamous poster of asylum seekers massed on the border. As Sivamohan Valluvan details, the nationalist rhetoric that vilified the immigrant and accused those on the left of putting the needs of refugees before those of native Britons ultimately led to the popularisation of the constituency of the 'left-behind', which 'alludes to a white working class that is understood as uniquely marginalised, and looks, accordingly, to rehabilitate certain anti-migrant and anti-minority attitudes that are discursively attributed to this constituency' (2019: 24–25). Even on the left, he argues, anti-immigration sentiment is too often read as 'a transparent grievance *authentically authored* by the forgotten (read: white) working class' (176 emphasis and parentheses in the original), a perspective that can be seen in the arguments, for example, of Simon Winlow and Steve Hall (2023) in *The Death of the Left.* This 'left-behind' narrative of grievance and injury, Valluvan asserts, invests the notion of the working-class subject with whiteness, 'and this whiteness is presented as being under threat from migration, political correctness, equalities politics and the very idea of a multi-ethnic society itself'(2019: 176).

This was a particular, and lethal, rhetorical manifestation of the return of the working-class subject, no longer as abject and multi-racial, but now as victim and white, a turn which, as Kirsteen Paton articulates, 'speaks less to the working class as unproductive, without value and responsible for their own hardships and more that they are the exclusive victims of government policies and have been "left behind" and overlooked by political representatives' (2024: 167). Such a turn not only neglects to acknowledge previous and existing evidence of multi-racial working-class solidarity (Virdee and McGeever, 2023: 143) and the disproportionate hardship experienced by minority ethnic groups through the years of austerity but also constitutes, as Valluvan warns, 'an incendiary racial nativism' (2019: 10).

There were, however, other class fractions which would not recognise themselves as 'left-behind' that Farage's populist movement had in its sights. Just as 'hard-working families' had pulled the aspirant working-class and lower-middle-class fractions together in a single rhetorical figure, so did Farage's preferred figure of 'ordinary people', as most famously expressed in his declaration that the majority vote for Leave was 'a victory for real people, a victory for ordinary people, a victory for decent people' (Nigel Farage, 24 June 2016).[19]

---

[19] While Virdee and McGeever are clear to point out that the two lowest social classes only made up 24 per cent of the overall proportion of those who voted for Leave, a strong majority (two-thirds) of those social classes did vote Leave, in addition to a significant percentage of the 'white-collar proletariat' and the 'skilled manual working class'. Thus, for Virdee and McGeever, 'the working class vote was indeed central to Brexit' (2023: 139).

Ordinary people, for Farage, are not the multi-racial aspirational working and lower middle classes that were hailed by New Labour as 'hard-working families', but the (implicitly white) working and lower middle classes, now including the unemployed.

The antagonist of the 'ordinary people' was, as in all populist narratives, figured as the 'elite'[20] who had been punished by the Brexit vote for their neglect of the economic plight of the 'left-behind' and the political concerns, especially regarding immigration, of 'ordinary people'. The seemingly banal descriptor 'ordinary' – especially when read alongside 'real' and 'decent' (see above) – does two important jobs for Farage. On the one hand, it creates a distinction between 'ordinary people' and a cultural, political, liberal or metropolitan 'elite' who are seen as 'not ordinary' by virtue of their economic, cultural and/or political privilege. On the other, it creates a distinction between 'ordinary (British/English) people' and racial outsiders who are perceived, in nationalist discourse, to be exceptional to the 'norm' of 'ordinary'/'authentic' (white) identity and heritage, to be 'not really British/English'. While Farage and those following him are rarely explicit that the 'ordinary people' they are hailing are white, the demonisation of asylum seekers lands more squarely, if not uniquely, on this constituency, given the diasporic heritages of many citizens of colour and the wider racial bigotry that hate-speech against asylum seekers so often invokes.[21]

The antagonist figure of the 'elite' is also slippery to pin down. Used in conjunction with 'political', it can encompass the most right-wing of Tory politicians, when employed to pull votes away from Conservative administrations and towards Farage's own party, Reform UK.[22] However, it most often has the cultural, and left-leaning, fraction of the middle class in its sights, especially when used in conjunction with liberal, metropolitan or cultural. This is the class fraction whose expressed political solidarity with asylum seekers and commitment to an anti-racist and decolonising agenda, as I will return to later in this subsection, can be most easily weaponised in Farage's hail to the 'ordinary people' he is inviting into his nationalist, populist movement. Farage's particular confection of this double-edged antagonism sowed the seeds for many variants of the populist narrative of 'elite' versus 'ordinary people' that grew and flourished in the right-wing press and increasingly right-wing political discourse in the years following Brexit. The figure of the cultural fraction of the middle class falls squarely into the rhetorical figure of

---

[20] See Ellis, 2022, and Tournier-Sol, 2021, for extended analysis of the role of the 'elite' in post-Brexit right-wing discourse.

[21] As seen in the attacks on hotels housing asylum seekers and on Mosques in the far-right riots of August 2024, supposedly in retribution for the stabbing of three young girls in Southport by someone who was neither an asylum seeker nor a Muslim.

[22] Reform UK, is a right-wing populist party, led by Nigel Farage since June 2024.

the elite which was, at times, explicitly referred to as a 'cultural elite' (Stanley, 2019 and 2021; Deacon, 2023), while in the right-wing tabloids, the term most commonly used was 'the woke brigade' (McKinstry, 2021 and 2023).

Accelerating acutely since 2015, this confected conflict, in all its guises, has been designed to encourage historically left-wing post-industrial working-class communities to abandon their traditional political allies in the cultural fraction of the middle class and vote against the latter's preferences to supplement the vote for the hard right – firstly for Leave, and subsequently for successive Conservative-led Governments or Reform UK. This operation has been undertaken, in the words of political scientist E. E. Schattschneider (1961), through a concerted 'mobilization of bias' by the political right, who have consistently argued into political discourse precisely those topics – immigration and national identity – that will best feed the class conflict they require (Schattschneider in Sobolewska and Ford, 2020: 121). While the binary nature of this conflict is sometimes speculative and overdetermined (see, for example, Goodhart, 2017; Winlow and Hall, 2023;) the impact of the multiple confected narratives of ideological hostility between a 'cultural elite' and 'ordinary people' has succeeded in consolidating real and lasting class and race antagonisms which are well-evidenced in empirical research.

The real ideological divisions underpinning Farage's rhetoric of class conflict are not new, as Evans and Tilley's (2017) study demonstrates. They identify a 'long-standing body of research that suggests that occupation and education matter', with a 'standard finding' that 'on a ladder of tolerance and liberalism, it is those in professional jobs, our new middle class, who are at the top, with the working class at the bottom' (2017: 69). Education, rather than occupation, is at the heart of Sobolewska and Ford's (2020) research, which uses levels of educational achievement rather than explicitly classed categories, to identify a comparable field of conflict. They evidence an ideological antagonism between 'conviction identity liberals' (comprising university graduates, into which cohort the cultural fraction of the middle class would mostly fall) and 'identity conservatives' (white school leavers without university qualifications, into which cohort the white working and lower middle class would mostly fall). This reflects the antagonism figured in more rhetorical terms between a 'cultural elite' and 'ordinary people' as outlined in this subsection. Sobolewska and Ford locate the central component of antagonism as the ethnocentric world view of the latter who 'are strongly prone to negative views of immigrants and tend to oppose policies which support and protect ethnic minorities' (62), and the commitment to anti-racism held by the former.[23] Virdee and McGeever's

---

[23] Sobolewska and Ford also identify a third tribe defined as "necessity identity liberals' (school leavers of colour without university qualifications) who most often, but not always, ally with the 'conviction identity liberals'. This strategic and partial alliance is based on the latter's

account of how 'racism played a formative role' (2023: 4–5) in the project of Britain's democratic settlement from the late nineteenth century onwards is useful to put Sobolewska and Ford's conclusions into a deeper context, as it demonstrates how ethnocentrism has been central to the capitalist interpellation of all British subjects throughout modern history. This suggests that, if critique of ethnocentrism is absent from the family and local community context (whatever the class), higher education is the environment in which such embedded ideology is most likely to be challenged, rather than the alternative reading that ethnocentrism is somehow essentially baked in to the class position of the white working class.

None of this is to say, of course, that such preponderances uncovered by empirical research, and strategically mobilised in political rhetoric, are the full story. There will always be significant numbers of individuals in all categories that do not align with the ideologies identified in the previous paragraph. Moreover, as Valluvan argues, there is growing sociological awareness of how 'convivial multiculture' (2019: 204) operates in working-class communities throughout Britain, *'in spite of* racialised nationalism' (205 original emphasis) in ways that might contest the long-term continuation of the political divides described above. The danger, of course, is that both sides of Farage's binary are seduced by the rhetorical *narrative* of the culture wars and hardened in their own identitarian role within it. This can consolidate and exacerbate both antagonisms noted above: that between the white working and lower middle class and precarious people of colour (especially asylum seekers); and that between the white working and lower middle class and the cultural fraction of the middle class. It is the second that most concerns us here, given the central role of the cultural fraction in the subsidised theatre industry that is the subject of this study.

2.5 Class Conflicts on the Theatre Stage

The two subsections above highlight how, through the rhetoric of successive governments, the figure of the working-class subject has been erased, stigmatised and racially weaponised over previous decades. The previous subsection also highlights how the allyship of the cultural fraction of the middle class for a non-white precariat in particular has been weaponised to create antagonism between this fraction and the white working- and lower-middle-class constituencies captured in the rhetorical figure of the 'ordinary people'. These narratives of class conflict provide the context for this Element's engagement with the subsidised

---

ideological commitment 'to protect vulnerable minorities from the ethnocentric hostility and discrimination they deplore' and to which the school leavers of colour are most often subjected (67). However, this group do not, for the most part, share the 'broader socially liberal agenda' (7) of the conviction identity liberals.

sector of the theatre industry, nestled at the very heart of the cultural fraction of the middle class. The first political operation, described above in 2.3, of the stigmatisation of the most precarious fraction of the working class, has provoked in the sector an impassioned counter-operation, as will be examined in Section 3, that seeks to stage the precarious subject in order to challenge the ideological imaginary of cultural and moral deficit perceived to be held by the theatre audience.

However, in Sections 4 and 5, I will ask if the ubiquity of the precarious protagonist, and the counter-operation undertaken, might play a role in limiting the cultural and discursive space in which protagonists from outside this alliance, of all ethnicities, might be permitted to share wider working- or lower-middle-class experiences, or offer different perspectives or values to those held by the cultural fraction of the middle class – perhaps even to oppose them. A cultural stage on which this can happen becomes particularly vital in light of the second political operation outlined above in 2.4, in which the cultural fraction of the middle class are painted as the enemy of the wider working and lower middle classes, especially those who are white. The cultural fraction of theatre artists and scholars must be vigilant to avoid the trap of accepting a confected populist narrative in which working- and lower-middle-class whites are assumed to hold the views that are attributed – implicitly or explicitly – to Farage's figure of the 'ordinary people'. A failure to avoid such a trap risks a conflation of the figure of the white working-class subject with a figure not of abjection but of dangerous racist recidivism which, as I argue in Section 5, conjures a re-directed ideological imaginary of moral and cultural deficit of the white working- and lower-middle-class fractions.

3 Staging the Ideological Imaginary of Deficit

This section will examine how the complex relationship between the cultural fraction of the middle class and the most precarious fraction of the working class is differently configured in three plays that explicitly stage antagonism, but also, at times, invite a complicated allyship between these class fractions.[24] In each play, the political strategy is to expose and challenge the ideological imaginary of deficit that mainstream narratives of stigmatisation and abjectification, as detailed in Section 2, have ascribed to the most precarious fractions of the working class. I will examine how this political strategy is designed to play out in Gary Owen's *Iphigenia in Splott* (2015), Kieran Hurley's *Mouthpiece* (2018) and Chris Bush's *Hungry* (2021).

There are strong similarities between the aims of the three plays, but most importantly I will signal distinctions that impact on the political strategy of

---

[24] An early draft of this section was presented at *Resisting Theatre: Plays, Politics and the Academy* University of York and Royal Holloway, University of London (18–21 June 2021).

each. In *Iphigenia* and *Mouthpiece*, I will argue that the aesthetic strategies are subversive: in each case they employ, what might be recognised by middle-class spectators as, tropes of abjection, signalling a moral and/or cultural deficit on the part of the white working-class protagonist, which is then decisively over-turned in the course of the narrative when great reserves of moral and/or cultural capacity are demonstrated. While both plays configure the audience as the middle-class antagonist, in *Iphigenia*, the audience is interpellated by Owen as a broader cross-section of the middle class, whereas, in *Mouthpiece,* the specific cultural fraction of the middle class is more precisely targeted.

In *Hungry*, I argue, the tropes of abjection are absent, and Bex, a working-class protagonist of colour, is portrayed with significant moral and cultural capital from the start – a strategy I define as resistant. This enables the protag-onist, rather than merely demonstrating her rejection of the identity of abjection to which she has been condemned, to reverse the terms of established class and racial hierarchies and claim her own cultural habitus as the place of value, in which not everyone is welcome. Nonetheless, the culmination of Bush's play not only throws this act of resistance into doubt but also questions the very possibility of overcoming an ideological imaginary that remains so firmly, if often unconsciously, embedded in the cultural space of the professional subsid-ised theatre.

3.1 Figures of Abjection

The mythical character of Iphigenia is reconfigured in Gary Owen's play as Effie (see Figure 1), a young girl from Splott, an inner-city Cardiff suburb which, as Stef Kerrigan asserts, 'is partly defined by its state of living ruin' (2022: n.p.), and is characterised by Owen through 'an inventory of eco-political, austerity-driven failures' (2022: n.p.). As well as the identification of place as an indicator of character, a factor also key to Katie Beswick's (2019) study of council estates in performance, Effie is explicitly constructed from the derogatory figuration of the white working-class 'chav' discussed in Section 2. All the familiar tropes of the abjectified subject so beloved of the right-wing press are present. Effie is 'skint' and without work. There are no parents, only a nan to whom Effie is rude and disrespectful. Effie is a regular drug user and excessive drinker. She presents as sexually promiscuous, she failed at school, and she is violent and abusive to passers-by on the street. In performance, Sophie Melville is aggressive and loud, at times directly confronting the audience. She liberally uses large confrontational gestures, and her physical momentum dominates the stage. She revels in the identities of 'slag' and 'skank' she knows the audience would impose on her if they met her in the street.

Figure 1 Sophie Melville as Effie in *Iphigenia in Splott*. Photograph
by Mark Douet.

If Effie is figured as the abjectified subject intended to disgust an audience
interpellated as middle class, Kieran Hurley's Declan is figured as a much more
sympathetic character. Although he has neither money nor job, Declan is shown
to be considerate of others, his greatest priority being the care of his younger
sister. Furthermore, he is a talented artist who is thrilled when introduced to the
work of Francis Bacon. Yet, Declan's characterisation explicitly draws on
a different white working-class trope to the abjectified figure of Effie: that of
the vulnerable child. As noted in Section 1, historical perceptions located the
poor closer to nature or infancy, and thus further from cultural capacity, than the
middle-class subject. These perceptions live on through the dominant ideological imaginary of the precarious subject that infantilises them and positions

Figure 2 Libby buys Declan a coke in *Mouthpiece*. Photograph
by Roberto Ricciuti.

them in need of not only approbation (as in Effie's case) but also care and
instruction. Declan's relationship with middle-class, late-thirties Libby further
reinforces his child-like, uncultured status with both class and age differences
being clearly marked. She buys him pencils to enable him to continue his
drawing, and takes him to the café for a coke and bacon roll while she drinks
coffee and prefers avocado with her bacon (see Figure 2). Declan is also figured
as semi-illiterate and ignorant of cultural norms, reading 'artisanal produce' as
'art is anal produce', and misunderstanding that the theatre is not free to enter in
the way that he has discovered art galleries are.

Effie is set up to inspire approbation and moral condemnation on the
part of the audience before the play invites the spectators to confront their
own prejudice. Declan is set up to inspire care and cultural instruction
from Libby, before exposing the audience's complicity in her cultural
effacement of him. Effie's figuration is designed to expose moral deficit,
Declan's to expose cultural deficit. In both cases, the narratives develop to
evidence that each character holds the capacity that their stigmatising
figurations had suggested was absent, and the audience are invited to
examine their own complicity in the assumptions that they might have
drawn from the figurations and tropes of precarity and abjection with
which they were presented.

3.2 Narratives of Subversion

In Effie's story, the revelation of moral capacity follows the death of her newborn child in an ambulance caught between hospitals in a snowstorm. Tempted by the probability of an NHS payout of over £277,000 for their neglect to provide her with a midwife to accompany her on the journey, Effie is persuaded otherwise by a conversation with the midwife, whose presence had been more forcibly demanded, on that night, by the articulate middle-class partner of another expectant mother:

> You were only in that ambulance cos
> We didn't have a special care bed left
> … Cos of all these cuts …
> She says if we pay you, we'll have to cut more.
> And more old people will die before they should.
> More young people will never get a chance to live.
> And more mums, just like you, will lose –
> I say I don't know what you're crying about, bitch – apart from your job.
>
> (Owen, 2015: 62–63)

But despite Effie's instinctively hostile response, she drops the case, because she knows the money cannot heal the pain, and that perhaps the knowledge that she has done something to help others, might.

> I took this pain,
> And saved every one of you, from suffering the same
> Your baby gets sick, she gets well
> Because of me. Your mum gets ill
> She gets healed, because of me and still:
> You see me, pissed first thing wandering home
> And all you think is, stupid slag. Nasty skank.
> When what you should be thinking is,
> Christ Effie, thanks. You took the cut, for all of us.
>
> (64)

And in this way the modern Iphigenia 'takes the cut' as a selfless sacrifice that might, ultimately, enable others to be saved.

In *Mouthpiece*, the figuration of Declan, as noted above, performs a different role. He is not lacking in moral capacity and is marked out by his ability to draw, but is hampered in any cultural aspirations by the barriers of his social class and context of his upbringing. For this reason, Hurley is already presenting this character as holding a cultural capacity that would challenge the ideological imaginary of deficit outlined above, and pointing to the systemic structures that will not permit Declan to break out of the figuration to which he appears to be condemned. Yet, Hurley's political intention is more sophisticated than leaving the blame at the door of societal structures from which the audience, and their stand-in, the character Libby, can easily distance themselves. Declan is infant-ilised, and ultimately exploited, by Libby, despite her own belief that she is helping him, and this, Hurley suggests, is the real danger of the ideological imaginary of deficit. It pervades even the best intentions of the cultural fraction of the middle class: people like Libby and those who Hurley assumes will make up the most part of the audience at the Edinburgh Traverse, where the play premiered, and in which the final scene is set.

Having 'withdrawn her consent' from their would-be sexual relationship, Libby tells Declan that the play she is writing based on the life-story he has been sharing with her is going down really well with 'some people at a theatre' (53). She also reveals, or rather Declan guesses, what happens to the main character in the play: 'So what, take a cunt like me right, make him top himsel cause ay the Bad Poverty. Tragedy. Poor cunt like me. And aw the cunts like *you* sit there and go "very sad, aye, very bad, tut tut, oh dear"' (53). Libby's adoption of the role of the teacher as she takes him through the rules of playwriting – a motif throughout the play – simply enrages him further:

> Declan   ... Ken what, you can fuck off then and say ta-ta to
>   your skanky 'project' cause I'm fucked if I'm letting you
>   use my story.
> Libby   Well. You can't just simply do that all of a sudden,
>   that's not –
> Declan   Fucking watch me. Here: I withdraw my consent. You
>   like that?
> Libby   Come on that's different. That is different.
> Declan   How?
>   *Beat*
> Libby   Because. This is my story now.

(55)

And in this line, Hurley encapsulates the exploitation. Declan is returned to his place. He may be a good, authentic life story of precarity for the profit of a middle-class playwright and her middle-class audience, but he is not an artist in his own right and is no longer required in the chain of commodification. Declan is consigned to silence, while his voice is appropriated and moulded into a cultural project, the play, the rules of which are placed beyond his compre-hension, just as the theatre which will support the play is assumed to be beyond his reach.

Whereas Effie's confrontation with the audience rests on her overturning their expectations of the moral deficit of her figuration, Declan's confrontation with Libby and the audience consists of a rejection of the infantilisation of his figuration, a collapsing of the assumption that he has no cultural capacity to use his own voice to tell his own story, or to challenge those who have appropriated it and exploited him. Despite never having been to a theatre before, he makes his way to the Traverse on the opening night. The 'real' theatre audience align with the fictional theatre audience for the final scene, in which Libby takes the stage for a talk-back after the fictional play has finished. And at this point, from his seat among the audience (which is now both real and fictional), Declan sticks up his hand to 'talk-back': 'Hiya ladies and gentlemen. Enjoying your drinks aye? Um. Hing is right. My name is Declan Swan and this play stole my life' (65). Declan goes on to demand a share of the £9,000 that Libby got for writing the play, so that he can provide for his little sister whom his mother has taken from him. But as Alba Knijff Massip proposes, Declan does not become a political subject at this point by claiming his rights to the economic or cultural profit of the play that resulted from Libby's appropriation but rather through, in Jacques Rancière's terms, a rupturing and redefinition of 'the field of experience' (Rancière, 1999: 40 in Knijff Massip, 9), in which the rules of the theatrical and social contracts are turned on their head.

This occurs as Libby tries to persuade him to leave the theatre to speak with her privately, but Declan begins to punch himself in the head, before holding a knife to his throat: 'Fucking telling me how tay act! Still! What happens now then eh? Writer? You decide' (68). At this point we see the play hand over the narrative power to Declan. As the projected text above the stage scrolls 'Declan violently thrusts the knife across his neck', the stage directions in the published playtext, followed in performance, read '*Declan, still screaming, does not thrust the knife across his neck*' (69). As Knijff Massip argues, prior to this rupture, 'Declan has no capacity for action' (6). It is not that 'a pre-constituted experience' has been 'ex-propriated from Declan'; rather the 'constitutive parameters' of Libby's authorship (which, I would argue, are intended to reflect the parameters of the cultural stage more widely) 'prevent his enunciation and, therefore, need to be reconfigured' (6). So, as the projected text of 'the writer' continues to detail Declan's death before the audience, the character himself narrates a different ending. Declan refuses to die the tragic death of the abjectified subject, just as he refuses to be silenced, and insists on literally taking the stage and 'talking-back' to those who had appropriated his story and his own voice.

3.3 Dramaturgies of Subversion

One danger in the repetition of the tropes of abjection that are employed in *Mouthpiece* and *Iphigenia* is that they recirculate, regardless of their eventual subversion, a familiar imaginary of the white working-class subject that risks two things. Firstly, it risks reducing the plurality of the working class to that of its most marginal fraction, the precariat. Secondly, it risks confirming the subject of abjection as a social reality, rather than the strategic and ideological confection discussed in Section 2. This second risk, in particular, makes it essential that the dramaturgies of characterisation offer the audience the opportunity for a critical re-positioning of the figurations that are presented. This is vital, as Katie Beswick argues, to avoid representations of working-class subjects becoming 'authenticating mechanisms for existing understandings of estate life' (2019: 90). Beswick is particularly concerned about the potential for this within the model of social realism, where there is arguably less dramaturgical capacity for meta-theatrical class analysis or critical reflection to be threaded through, or to comment on, the narrative itself.

A key strategy that enables this critical reflection is the subversion of both social realist dramatic conventions and existing social hierarchies by permitting the characters themselves to speak back to the audience gaze. In her analysis of *Road* and *Les Misérables*, Jenny Hughes (2015) identifies the figure of the trickster and argues that characters such as Scullery (in *Road*) and Thénardier (in *Les Misérables*) are able to mobilise a critical theatricality 'to carve out niches for human encounters that unsettle the fixing frames of spectatorship' (17). Tricksters can, on the one hand, disrupt the framework of the stage world in which the represented subjects are contained, 'traversing the worlds of the play [...] and communicating directly with audiences' (17), but they can also reject their capture by sociological and ideological classification given that they 'revel in abjection and refuse work, including work on the self, other than the work it takes to appear in disguise and unsettle appearances' (17). Like Hughes' trickster, Effie and Declan address the audience directly, and explicitly hold up the audience's potential classification of them as abject for critical examination: Effie, from the start, and Declan from the point at which he takes over the narrative and begins to act against it. They are the 'troublemakers' in Savran's words, who are 'always threatening to undo the very binary oppositions they secure' (Savran, 2003: x in Hughes, 2015: 14).

In addition to this departure from the fourth wall of social realism, different modes of acting are also used strategically in *Iphigenia* to drive through the political operation of subversion. Sophie Melville's virtuoso performance of Effie is predominantly reminiscent of director Steven Berkoff's style: grotesque, highly physically-charged, with liberal, choreographic use of gesture and movement that enables a stylised and larger-than-life characterisation. Melville's vocal work is equally pronounced. Owen's poetic dialogue is delivered in a rapid-fire monologue, with notably physical use of the mouth that gives the impression of carnality and enables sneers that are more sculpted than naturalistic. Melville's highly technical performance thus inspires admiration for the virtuosity of the actor, as the character simultaneously repels, and this enables the character, Effie, to vicariously claim, through Melville, a level of expertise and skill that contrasts with her abjectified figuration. Melville, the actor, is most present in the moments when Effie is at her worst: the 'skank', it seems, is permitted expertise in her self-portrayal of 'skank', and that particular identity is emphasised as performative, ultimately constructed out of the stigmatising figuration of herself by others. As Sean McEvoy observes in relation to Jez Butterworth's work, when 'class is self-consciously performed in the theatre' it can make '"ordinary" characters appear at home on the stage of the Royal Court or of the Almeida; they are not specimens brought in for examination from outside'. In this way 'the class-superiority of theatrical performance culture is undermined' (2021: 11).

Melville's grotesque characterisation is not, however, the whole story. If it were, the danger might not be a realistic reconfirmation of the abjectified residents of *Benefits Street* but a reflection of the Vicky Pollard character from *Little Britain*, a cruel satire of the precarious for the humour of those more privileged. To prevent this, there are key moments when the 'performance of skank' falls away, and a mode of naturalistic performance takes over, where the part is played as if for real. Here we see the inner self of Effie; her amazement at her love for Lee, a soldier with whom she shares only one night but believes she will be with forever; her empathy for Lee and his daughter when she cannot, in the end, bring herself to confront him in front of his wife and child; and, ultimately, the love she has for her own child, that no money can replace. Key moments where we shift to this different Effie are marked by subtle sound effects and lighting changes, but they are never sentimental; the audience are barely permitted in before Owen's text pulls the audience back to humour. Having headed to Lee's house to expose him and his treatment of her as a disposable one-night stand, she sees him lift his little girl high in the air, and there is a rare sound effect, a gentle gong, as she continues softly, 'She shouts, / *Daddy!* / And I remember / I remember shouting like that' (38), but this moment of sheer pathos, given the absence of parents in Effie's life, is immediately cut down: 'And – / And the wife says to me, / Sorry, can I help you? / Because I am standing on their drive' (38). The accompanying shift in Melville's delivery causes the audience to laugh,[25] but there is more.

I see her eyes close
I see her lips move and though I don't hear
I know what she's saying
She's saying
Daddy
And I remember
I remember
sorry, you wanted what? the wife goes.
I say
fuck –
I say
Yeah I'm just trying to find my way back to Grand Avenue?

(39)

The 'daddy' here is delivered in such a high pitch that it is almost inaudible, but Owen's text and Melville's performance keep such glimpses into Effie's inner self rare. What this shifting mode of performance intends is that the audience realise throughout the piece that the 'skank' Effie, the familiar abjectified subject from poverty porn tropes, is the performance that Effie constructs to keep the 'real' Effie hidden. This 'skank' is not authentic at all, an authenticity which is exposed as a mere copy of the mythology of the trope of abjection, but rather the 'character' that Effie adopts in line with what is expected of her – not only by the other characters in the play but, critically, she anticipates, by the theatre audience: 'And all you think is, stupid slag. Nasty skank' (64). But underneath the performance of that character, there is another character who is able to transcend the limitations of her figuration – a character who demonstrates her moral capacity to be able to 'take it' for other people. 'I can take it', she says as she walks away from Lee and his family, 'So I do take it / For that little girl' (39) – a foreshadowing of what she is finally asked by the midwife to 'take' for her own little girl and, subsequently, the cut she takes for all of those who might still, when seeing her walk down the street, close their eyes to her 'real' character of value, and choose to see only the surface performance of 'skank'.

3.4 Interpellating the Audience

Both the direct address form of the monologue and the explicit nature of Effie's charge to the audience configure the spectator as complicit in both the stigmatisation of Effie and the neoliberal state of austerity which asks those who can least afford it to suffer the most pain. Rebeca Gualberto argues that 'the audience, addressed directly, is forced to see the violence of the system that guarantees their wellbeing . . . and then to respond with shame and guilt when they realise that Effie is right' (2021: 130). However, my contention, as discussed in Section 2, is that the cultural fraction of the middle class, who make up the most part of subsidised theatre audiences, is rarely characterised by the kind of right-wing politics that would have supported the Conservative-led govern- ment's austerity measures. Indeed, they are more likely to hold left-wing, pro- welfare views aligned to those of Owen himself that fuel outrage at the suffering the cuts to public services have caused. This is not to say that all those holding such politics would welcome Effie into their own home, or that they would not react in precisely the way she understands, were they to see her walking down the street, but it does cast doubt on whether they would willingly recognise themselves in the figure who stood accused by the play. Such recognition would be essential for the 'shame and guilt' that Gualberto assumes would be the outcome of the play's political operation, but Owen's exposure of the unjust stigmatisation of the precariat by the middle class and the charge, to the latter, of complicity with the cruel politics of neoliberalism seem to interpellate a middle- class fraction of a more socially and economically right-wing persuasion than empirical evidence suggests is likely to have been the case.

Mouthpiece, conversely, interpellates its audience more precisely as the cultural fraction of the middle class. Libby provides the on-stage representation of this class fraction, standing in for the audience as the antagonist of the precarious figure of Declan. While there is never any sense of allyship between Effie and her audience (her tragedy is that she is entirely without allies through- out the play), Libby professes an allyship for the disenfranchised that is designed to resonate with the cultural fraction of the middle class who are anticipated to make up the most part of the audience. Yet, this allyship is shown to be an unequal alliance – at best a delusion, at worst a strategy, which quickly turns into the exploitation and commodification of Declan as an 'authentic life of precarity' that can be appropriated and employed for Libby's cultural and economic advancement.

However much any spectator might attempt to disidentify with the crime of the artist in *Mouthpiece*, Hurley's inventive dramaturgy captures them inescapably in role as the fictional audience complicit in the act and makes it difficult to escape the question of whether they are, or have ever been, guilty of complicity in acts of artistic or cultural appropriation of this kind. The challenge Hurley throws at the audience is to critically reflect on how their attitudes and behaviour, however well-intentioned, towards those figured as Declan, might mirror the infantilisation and exploitation enacted by Libby. When Declan observes in horror that 'They even got a wee fucking ginger cunt tae play me, I'm no fucking ginger man, fucksake! (63), we are faced with the conundrum of an actor playing the 'real' Declan who is challenging the 'fictional' actor who is playing the 'real' (in the fiction) Declan. When he dismissively notes that the 'wee arsehole who plays me pipes up – honestly he's been speaking like me for the last hour and a half, pipes up noo in this wee chirpy cunty voice and says it's very "meta'" (64), it is impossible not to wonder if this actor, too, has a 'wee chirpy cunty voice' that is nothing like the one we are hearing. More significantly, we wonder whether we are witnessing Hurley doing his own version of the act with which Libby is being charged or whether we, like the fictional audience, are equally guilty of the kind of cultural mission that Declan accuses them of: 'it's all fucking very well wanting to be a voice for the voiceless eh. Until you find oot the voiceless have a fucking voice and mibbe they might want tae use it' (66). The play does not rest merely on overturning the stigmatising narrative of the abjectified subject who is now empowered to speak back but challenges the audience to question the role they might be playing in the cultural appropriation of such a voice, and the silencing of it. Hurley's piece is fictional; there is no 'real' Declan whose voice is being appropriated here, but the fiction is, nevertheless, a self-critical challenge that demands attention to cultural products that stage precarious subjects for the cultural benefit of a predominantly middle-class audience – a trend that will be the focus of Section 4.

3.5 Resistance and Reversal

Chris Bush's *Hungry* centres on an inter-class, inter-racial love affair that develops, and finally implodes, between Lori, a white chef in her late twenties/early thirties, and Bex, a twenty-two-year-old woman of colour who first meets Lori as a temporary member of her waiting staff. The age and professional status dynamics between Bex and Lori could mirror the relationship between Declan and Libby, but the significant departure from abjectification in the way that Bex's classed identity is configured enables, I will argue, a very different conversation with the audience to take place. Where Declan's choice of coke and bacon was unselfconscious, and his misreading of 'artisanal' was unintentional, Bex uses her liking of junk food, such as pot noodles and chicken nuggets, to deliberately provoke Lori, and her insistence on characterising 'basil fluid gel' as 'green gunk ... dribble round the edge' (2021: 12) is also entirely knowing and deliberate. Bex, from the opening of the play, is aware of how the ideological imaginary of cultural deficit functions and how she herself will be figured by it. Moreover, she uses her knowledge to keep one step ahead of Lori, as she weaponises the imaginary of deficit to humorous effect. It appears, in the first scene, that Bush is setting her up for the audience as culturally deficient – if not stupid – as Bex seemingly misunderstands Lori's instructions about placing the spoon at 2 o'clock when serving the plate:

> Bex: (*glancing at her watch*) It's nine-thirty.
>   . . .
> Lori: Seriously? (*Sighs*) Okay, so a clockface – picture
>   a clockface –
> Bex: Why?
>   . . .
> Lori: Big hand! Big hand at –
> Bex: Thing is I'm more digital.
> Lori: It isn't –
> BEX   *can't keep this up any longer. She cracks up.*
> BEX: Your face. (9)

Here, Bex deliberately plays stupid so that an audience laughing at the humorous dialogue is light-heartedly wrong-footed by the playwright, as Bex exposes that she has been in charge of the joke from the start. Her character, played by Melissa Lowe in the 2022 Edinburgh performance I attended, is consistently given the wittiest lines throughout the play, and most often had the audience laughing with her at Lori as she undercut, with deadpan delivery, many of Lori's more middle-class assumptions:

> Lori: And you can do what you want with . . . Chuck all the . . .
>   Or don't, actually – give it to some homeless –
> Bex: No homeless person wants a pulled-jackfruit wrap. (50)

The humour gets darker once we see Lori introduce her grand vision for them both: to own a restaurant that turns away from, what Lori dismisses as, the more pretentious side of fine dining, to serve 'Soul Food' that draws on 'traditions, not trends': 'Not junk – still healthy and eco-conscious and sustainable, just without making a big deal about it. Big flavours – bright, fresh, punchy' (43). Lori goes on to list 'a jambalaya, or a jollof, or a jerk whatever' for Bex to respond acerbically, 'Okay. None of those things are Soul Food though' (43). The charge that Lori is ignorantly exoticising the cultural traditions of the diaspora to which Bex belongs is one that is clearly valid, given her comment that Bex is needed as front of house to ensure that she doesn't get accused of doing precisely that. The language of the white middle-class coloniser also gives Lori away, even when she attempts an ostensibly decolonising discourse:

> Lori: . . . white chefs *should* be learning, we *should* be looking
>   further afield . . . studying all those world cuisines banished to
>   the deep-fat fryer and the late-night takeaway. And – and –

okay, if you look at some of those cultures, those, um, people
of specific ethnic backgrounds where there's a propensity
towards, uh, obesity, or diabetes, or heart disease – what if
that's because historically those cuisines have been neg-
lected? What if we take them, elevate them, do something
lighter, fresher, a bit different –

Bex: You want to teach my grandma how to fry chicken? (44–45)

Lori's exploitation of Bex on a personal level comes to a climax at the funeral of
Bex's mother when, despite Bex's clear instructions to leave the catering to her
family, Lori arrives with a series of new, and unsuitable, dishes to test proof of
concept for her new venture. This represents the turning point in the narrative
for Bex, but unlike the portrayals of Effie and Declan, there is no abjection here
to overturn. Rather than assert her right to claim cultural or moral value in
a classed and raced habitus that has abjected her, Bex instead claims her own
classed and raced space as the authoritative place of value and rejects Lori as the
unwelcome outsider, telling her, 'you don't get to sit with us. You don't belong
at this table and you never will. That's okay. But it's enough now' (48).

Bush's play does not, then, seek to subvert the stigmatisation of the precarious working class subject, so much as it resists the operation of abjectification
altogether. Likewise, the assumptions underpinning the ideological imaginary
of cultural deficit, which centre white, middle-class cultural values as those to
be aspired to, are also resisted. This is reflected in Bex's refusal of the
trajectory of social mobility, proposed by Lori as a means of overcoming
her stigmatised figuration and proving her worth to gain a place at Lori's table.
Lori, rather, is figured as the one who has failed to assimilate into the
cultural values of Bex's habitus that she neither understands nor accepts as
legitimate.

While no firm conclusions can be drawn from a comparative analysis of the
three playtexts I have chosen to examine in this section, I suggest that it is not
incidental that the tropes of abjection, employed to initially characterise the
white working-class figures in *Mouthpiece* and *Iphigenia*, were not utilised in
the characterisation of Bex, a working-class figure of colour. Subsequent to the
Black Lives Matter resurgence in the summer of 2020, there has been significant
and rapid progress, within the creative subset of the cultural fraction of the
middle class, to address systemic and institutional racist practice, the under-
representation of people of colour in the cultural field and the importance of
decolonising all aspects of cultural life from university curricula to museum
curation. The impact of the BLM movement would make it politically ques-
tionable for a white playwright to present a mostly white audience with an

abjectified protagonist of colour (however much this was to be overturned in the process of the piece). Such developments, I would argue, suggest similar political caution might now be taken in the staging of abjectified white figures of precarity by and for the cultural fraction of the middle-class, regardless of political intention.

The decolonisation agenda has also significantly discredited, in the white cohort of this fraction of the middle class (or at least in their own self-evaluation), any ideological imaginary that negated or denied the existence and importance of black culture, along with all other global majority cultures and histories. This is, perhaps, what steers the play towards an ending in which Lori is forced to leave the metaphorical table which Bex claims as her own. This reversal enables Bush to avoid the risks of abjectification noted in 3.3, but there is a final shock in place for the audience: one that overturns not the ideological imaginary, but the myth that it might be so easily challenged. Having rejected Lori, Bex then undertakes a lengthy monologue in which she addresses the politics that underpin the ideological imaginary: identifying the 'class warfare' (55) that teaches the poor to know their place and only eat nuggets, and satirising Lori's 'wet dream of gentrification' (56) where they own a 'culturally insensitive neighbourhood restaurant ... all micro herbs and community gardens and pride flags and Stormzy on the playlist' (55). However, most damning of all, she identifies how this imaginary lies unconsciously at the very heart of Lori's love for her:

> You want me to blossom into something else and I think that's love –
> I genuinely think it is – but it's not reasonable. Love is unreasonable,
> maybe, but I just want to feel like enough, and I don't – not when I'm with
> you. I feel like I'm failing, and that was you. It's not me, it's you. And if
> I can't find a way to love you and love myself at the same time then I know
> what I have to do, because this can't be what it should feel like. Like I'm
> always having to hold my breath when I'm around you .... I'll be fine. I'm
> young. I'm smart. I'm hot. I was always enough – that was your mistake ....
> You can't fix something that isn't broken. I refuse to break. (56)

In this way, Bex identifies and debunks the ideological imaginary that locates the working-class subject as the subject of deficit, the subject who has tried and failed to attain middle-class status. But the definitive insight of the piece comes as Lori responds to this three-page diatribe with 'Bex? Are you okay? You haven't said anything for a really long time' (56). Because as Bex herself admitted in the course of what is now revealed to have been an inner, unspoken stream of consciousness, 'And I'm not saying things aren't shit – my life isn't shit – but it doesn't mean .... Aaargh! I can see the argument – it's there – it's flickering, but I can't quite ... '(53). Because Bex might possess the intelligence, the insight and the self-confidence to grasp the ideological argument, but what she is not permitted to do, by Bush, as by society, is to articulate it to a middle-class interlocutor or public. Here, the dramaturgy tells us that the Bex who is speaking these words, on a stage of high cultural capital to an audience who also hold such capital, is a dramatic device. In the play's reality, the working-class figure is not speaking out and, by extension, Bush suggests, their voice will never really, on the cultural stage that belongs to the middle class, be permitted to be heard.

This presents the spectators with the most difficult challenge of the work examined in this section. They can side-step the accusations of Effie, through disidentification with an audience who might have been misrecognised as more complicit with neoliberal ideology than they feel themselves to be; they can acknowledge the dangers of artistic commodification of the working-class voice and story, and pledge to be aware of this, and avoid it, in their own artistic practice and consumption; and they can do likewise in relation to Lori's colonialist appropriation of other cultures. But the final challenge that *Hungry* mounts is that the ideological imaginary of cultural deficit is not something that can be so simply recognised and avoided but an absorbed and unconscious reality that permeates not only the cultural fraction of the middle class but also those who are figured, and stigmatised, by it, even in a relationship that strives to overcome class and race differences through love.

In just the same way as critical race theory moved, within the cultural fraction of the middle class, from an admonition of explicit racist assumptions and behaviour to the necessity to confront an unconscious bias and race privilege that could not be so easily eradicated, it is now time for the critique of explicit stigmatisation of the working-class subject to give way to deeper questions. Can value be afforded to working-class cultures of all ethnicities, as it is now beginning to be celebrated in global majority cultures, rather than insisting, as Lori does, that the working-class subject has no culture of worth and must rather realise their capacity to become worthy of a place at the table of the cultural fraction of the middle class? Rather than challenging explicit class shaming of the precarious, a practice which is likely to be rare among the cultural fraction given their political leanings, how might we rather challenge an embedded class prejudice that ultimately ensures that regardless of social mobility for some individuals, the current cultural hierarchy and the class privilege within it remain unchanged. In the following section, I will examine how such a cultural hierarchy can remain undisturbed or consolidated, even when artists of working-class origin are invited onto the stage to tell their own stories.

4 Artists and Agency

There might seem to be no more conclusive challenge to the ideological imaginary of working-class cultural deficit than the working-class-origin artist who is given control of the literal stage to tell their own story on their own terms.[26] However, as noted in Section 2, any demographic widening of the creative subset of the cultural fraction to encompass more working-class-origin artists does not, in and of itself, enable those minoritised in the cultural sector by their class origin to control or determine the cultural tastes or aesthetic parameters favoured by the middle-class-origin majority and a middle-class theatre-going public. Moreover, the pervasiveness of all such ideological imaginaries of deficit, as the character Bex was clearly aware, is that they can be as easily internalised by those who are their target, as those who wield them.

In this section I will turn my attention to the working-class figures created and performed by working-class-origin artists, and the performer-audience antagonisms that are evoked in this heightened context. Precisely because the cultural and political mainstream narratives of stigmatisation are most often authored by those who are not of the communities they misrepresent, the authenticity of the lived experience of the working-class-origin artist becomes a strong validation of the counter-narratives offered. This authenticity is at its most explicit in autobiographical, or autofictional, performances, in which the artist whose lived experience is being narrated ostensibly overlaps with the protagonist who is telling that story on the stage.

While upholding the potential political currency of such dramaturgies, it remains the case that any repetition of the precarious, and sometimes abjectified, figure, utilised by artists to set up, then overturn, existing stigmatising tropes of deficit can, as examined in the previous section, risk perpetuating the dominance of such tropes, consolidating the myth that abjection is a social reality and reducing the plurality of the working class to a singular figuration of precarity in the imaginary of a mostly middle-class audience. This danger is indeed exacerbated when the singular figuration of precarity is authenticated by the autobiographical framing of it as the actual lived experience of the protagonist themselves. As Katie Beswick has argued in the context of social realism,

> the notion of authorial authenticity, especially when aimed at audiences unfamiliar with the estate environment, can result in authentic voice plays being framed as unproblematically 'real'. This imbues the work with an added burden of representation, as the stage depiction operates to solidify

---

[26] An early draft of this section was presented at the Theatre and Performance Research Association conference on 6–10 September 2021.

existing understandings about estates and is often read as reflecting the authentic totality of estate experience. (2019: 85)

In addition to the risk that the 'truthfulness' implied by the lived experience of the artist can be extended beyond any one singular account to stand in for working-class experience more broadly, this section will also propose a second risk, this time to the artist themselves. In dialogue with Arinzé Kene's *Misty* and Scottee's *Class*, I will examine how the cultural appetite of each show's audience is assumed, by the artists, to require that the first-hand accounts of working-class lived experience are shaped by tropes of precarity, and sometimes abjection, just as Hurley's fictional account of Libby's exoticisation of Declan's life in the previous section made clear. As a result, the danger is that the working-class-origin artist gains access to the cultural stage not principally as an artist valued for their craft but as a classed, and sometimes raced, figure valued only for the authenticity of their lived experience of precarity that can be transformed into an exoticised commodity for the audience. This reconfigured imaginary of cultural deficit is recognised and acknowledged in Scottee's autobiographical performance of *Class* and explicitly challenged in Arinzé Kene's autofictional play *Misty*, yet neither piece seems confident that working-class-origin artists are ever able to entirely evade capture by this particular manifestation of the ideological imaginary of cultural deficit that both artists are aiming to disrupt.

4.1 Commodification and Authenticity

The metatheatrical framework of *Misty* ostensibly explores the lived experience of the working-class-origin playwright/performer of colour, as he attempts to write the play that he wants to write, while fighting pressure from political and cultural interventions on all sides. The play within the play that the character 'Arinzé' is developing is a play about Lucas, a young black man from a background that bears all the tropes of an impoverished, violent, inner-city estate. Initially, he is categorised by Arinzé as the virus who exists among the – implicitly white – blood cells of the city, who violently attacks a fellow passenger on the bus, who later dies, leading to Lucas's attempts to evade the police hunt that ensues. Immediately after this opening, we hear voicemail messages from Arinzé's friends furiously cataloguing their issues with his story of another 'Generic angry young black man' (Kene, 2018: 17). These off-stage voices from the black community condemn his play as 'another "hood" story' (45) / 'an *urban* play' / 'a nigga play so your work would get on' / 'a modern minstrel show' (18), making the point that the audience who didn't 'look like us' (17) seemed to love it. Arinzé's comically precocious ten-year-old sister is given a theorised diatribe, warning her brother of the dangers of pandering 'to the voyeuristic needs of the bourgeoisie' (32) through his repetition of the stigmatising representations of young black men much loved, it is implied, by mostly middle-class, mostly white, theatre audiences.

In her study of representations of the council estate, Katie Beswick likewise cautions against the commodification of working-class voices which can be marketed as authentic accounts of an exoticized 'reality' which is far from the middle-class audience's own. Beswick and Lynette Goddard both comment on the dangers of theatre industry structures which limit opportunities for working-class playwrights, and playwrights of colour, to write about their life experience only in ways that 'reinforce dominant conceptions of inner-city life' (Beswick, 2019: 88). Beswick notes that 'repeatedly representing young black men as drug dealers and gangsters on stage, on screen and in the newspaper press can serve to suggest that young black men are "naturally" inclined towards crime and violence' (62). Lynette Goddard furthermore identifies the culpability of programmers and commissioners of work by black artists in the relentless repetitions of 'black teenagers and criminality', raising the possibility that 'mainstream presence was being achieved through stereotypical representations of urban black masculinity and "black-on-black" violence' (2015: 33). Furthermore, Goddard cites critic Darcus Howe's accusation that Roy Williams' play *Fallout* 'was not a slice of real life, but of low life sketched by the playwright for the delectation of whites' (Howe, 2003 in Goddard, 2015: 34).

In *Misty*, the character Arinzé calls on the justification of real-life experience to defend himself against the accusations of his friends and his sister. The play within the play, Arinzé initially informs us, is the true story of a young black man he interviewed, and he validates his telling of it on the familiar grounds that the personal is political: Lucas wanted his story to be told in order that people might hear the truth of it from his own lived experience. Yet, Arinzé's friend Raymond counters: 'It doesn't make it okay to tell a story, cos it's true' / 'some black writers "conveniently" wanna write narratives that majority white audiences are interested in seeing about black people' (2018: 44). Kene highlights, through the arguments of characters such as Raymond, the danger that certain accounts of marginalised lived experience, regardless of their truth value, will be exoticised and commodified by a predominantly white, middle-class audience, and thus shore up existing prejudices of spectators who have limited experience of the realities of black, working-class life.

4.2 Assimilation or Autonomy

Despite the weight of evidence against him, the character of Arinzé continues to defend himself against the accusations of Raymond (which echo the concerns of Beswick and Goddard) that his play is a 'modern minstrel show'. He responds with the anger of the artist who feels that he is being unfairly burdened with politicised requirements for representation that would not be expected of an artist who was neither of colour nor working class:

> I just. I write. I just wanna write my shit unencumbered. ... I don't even *wanna* write the enlightening play that ticks all the boxes and bridges the racial and sexual and LGBT abyss, that some people expect of me .... Can't it just be a play? Can a play from a person like me just be a fucking play already? Can we just hurry up and stop being weird about people like me writing plays and shit? (57–58)

Why, Kene asks here, should the artist from culturally minoritised communities be held to account for the stories they choose to tell, and/or the ways they choose to tell them? Why should the working-class-origin artist, which, for Kene, intersects with his being an artist of colour, be confined to being a politically productive voice for their specific community, rather than enjoying the freedom that artists from white, middle-class backgrounds take for granted? Through the conflict he establishes between Arinzé and Raymond, Kene seemingly sets up an uncomfortable binary choice for the working-class-origin artist of colour. He either 'defecat[es]' on his community (27), by offering perjorative representations of abjection authenticated through claims to real-life experience, or he is required to carry the burden of representation on behalf of his community by sacrificing the autonomy of his artistic vision to the imperative of constructing representations that will challenge the ideological imaginary of deficit.

However unpalatable this choice appears to be, it is not, as it happens, Kene's final word on the matter, because the binary conflict he identifies in Arinzé's speech above, between the politics of producing representations that will benefit the collective and the politics of access, agency and autonomy that will benefit the individual artist, is, he knows, a false one. Arinzé's sister is given the clearest argument that questions the degree of his autonomy as a working-class-origin artist of colour to write whatever he wants. She patiently explains that the 'psychosocial engineering programme' (32), which corresponds to the ideological imaginary of deficit discussed throughout this Element, 'engenders in our people feelings of self-doubt, self-hatred, and when that's what you're feeling, you could totally make up stories like, well, the one you seem to be writing right now' (33). The character Arinzé may believe he is writing the play he wishes to write, but the playwright Kene is ultimately clear that he may be dancing to invisible strings by so doing. Kene's concern, and one I share, is whether certain real-life stories, regardless of political intention, are unconsciously playing to just such an ideological imaginary: to the gallery of a cultural hegemony in which the value of working-class-origin artists lies not in any claim to artistic, imaginative or cultural capacity such as that granted to the artist from a middle-class background but entirely in their own 'natural', or 'embodied' lived experience which can be commodified and exoticised for audiences who wish to gain access to the authentic precarity of the other.

Such a reading raises alarming echoes, acutely so for working-class people of colour, of the 'noble savage' myths of the early twentieth-century avant-garde, where people of colour in colonized countries were perceived as free from cultural or material contamination and valued and exoticised for lives that were perceived as embodying the more 'natural' aspects of humanity. It also proposes a different direction taken by the ideological imaginary of cultural deficit within the theatre industry today, by implicitly proposing that the 'lived experience' of a working-class-origin artist is their primary, if not only, cultural asset within an aesthetic landscape that remains dominated by middle-class-origin cultural norms. While the relentless popularity of autobiographical performance as a form more widely is clearly driven by other cultural trends – notably the rise of the confessional in social media, the neoliberal emphasis on the commodification of the self and – in material terms – the comparative affordability of a one-person, direct-address show in the context of decade-long cuts to arts budgets, the implications of the form for working-class-origin artists might be seen to hold particular concerns.

In his study *The Philosopher and His Poor*, Jacques Rancière (2003) traces the ubiquity of the figure of the shoemaker through the philosophies of Plato, Marx and Bourdieu. Rancière argues that, as stand-in for the worker more widely, the importance of the shoemaker to philosophy resides in the fact that he is consigned to only ever do one thing: make shoes. If he is 'being' a worker, then he cannot simultaneously 'be' anything else, such as a poet or philosopher. His identity is, in fact, bound up in his capacity to make shoes only, and for him to attempt to move beyond this identity is seen as the greatest threat to the philosopher, whose monopoly on 'thinking', and the intellectual habitus in which this legitimately occurs, is sustained by all other 'workers' remaining outside of this habitus and within their allocated place in the social order. This allegory highlights the risk of working-class autobiographical performance serving as a form in which the working-class-origin artist is valued for only one thing: the authenticity of their life story of precarity, not their cultural capital to contribute aesthetically in ways that do not rely on the given of their biographical origins but on artistic capacities which are considered equal to those of artists from differently classed backgrounds. As Lianna Mark argues, 'the right to fictionalisation is, in short, inversely proportional to the requirement to be authentic. One's entitlement to the former and freedom from the latter depend on one's place on a spectrum from privilege to marginalisation, linked to race, class, gender, sexuality, and (dis)ability' (2024: 28). Kene's argument in *Misty*, voiced by Arinzé's sister, is that the artist themselves may believe that they are telling the story they want to tell, but it is difficult to extricate this desire from a structural imaginary of cultural deficit which the working-class artist may, themselves, have internalised.

If the autofictional figure of Arinzé remains compromised, and ultimately defeated, by this conundrum, the writer-actor Kene, as we saw in the work of Owen and Hurley in Section 3, employs dramaturgical subversions to assert the aesthetic value of his craft. The ostensibly autobiographical account of the playwright's ostensibly documentary biography of Lucas, validated on the grounds of voicing marginalised lived experience, is ultimately revealed to be a figment of the writer's imagination. Likewise, the authenticating mechanisms that initially underpin the autobiographical elements of Arinzé's story are constructed only to be systematically dismantled in an implicit defence of the artist's craft of fiction over authenticity. The names of Arinzé's friends, Donna and Raymond, are used for quite different characters in the prologue to the playtext than in the play itself, and are played, in performance, by the musicians. So, the reality of his friends who are evoked, and of his sister, who is clearly not speaking the words of a ten-year-old, is likewise destabilised, as is the reality of his producer who is voiced entirely by soundbites of Morgan Freeman. The story of Lucas himself is told through music and poetry and woven through the metaphor of a virus in the white blood cells of the city's arteries. An absurd motif of balloons, sometimes filled with water, or with orange powder, or enclosing the performer himself, runs through the piece to offer a further layer of visual and physical metaphor for the pressures the writer is under (see Figure 3). All these dramaturgical strategies distance the story not only from social realism but from the authenticating mechanisms of the autobiographical form it ostensibly assumes. In so doing, Kene insists explicitly on his aesthetic and creative capacities as an artist, rejecting the imaginary of cultural deficit that might recognise his value merely in his capacity to authenticate, for his audience, the abjectified tropes of black, working-class existence.

Figure 3 Arinzé Kene as 'Arinzé' in *Misty*. Photograph by Helen Murray/
ArenaPAL.

4.3 The Cost of Abjection

In Scottee's *Class*, the artist himself closes with a reflection on his own choice to stage an autobiographical narrative characterised by precarity, asking himself and the audience 'is this a working-class artist's only means of survival? To be laid bare?' (Scottee, 2020: 34). Throughout the piece, Scottee has recalled the often-traumatic experiences of his formative years growing up on an inner London council estate to shock and discomfort his audience with revelations about the reality of the lives lived by working-class people like him. Although there is plenty of humour in the show, the same material is often later twisted to something much darker. 'I was robbed at knifepoint on my estate aged 12. I started binge drinking at 13. I lost my virginity in a communal bin shed ... you laughed at that earlier?! Why's that not funny any longer?' (30). Throughout the piece the emphasis is on narratives of pain, dispossession, violence, homophobia, misogyny, addiction, destitution, junk food and bad television, and it culminates in Scottee's sharing of a photo-album, accompanied by the traumatic stories of the lives of those who appear there, much of which is redacted from the published script for reasons of sensitivity. Thus, Scottee's own story, while based on fact and designed to elicit an empathetic response from its audience, is nonetheless framed through narratives and images that are, at times, difficult to distinguish from the narratives and images of abjectified precarity that dominate mainstream representations of the poor, operating on a binary that swings between violence and victimhood. Moreover, there is a conflation in *Class* of Scottee's own personal narrative of precarity and the working class more broadly. Unlike the use of lived experience in social policy, whereby a plurality of narratives can reveal 'clusters of commonality and shared intersubjective experiences' (McIntosh and Wright, 2019: 459), the autobiograph-ical narrative is, by its nature, singular and subjective, and must not be presented, or taken, in Beswick's words, 'as reflecting the authentic totality of estate experience' (2019: 85). While the introduction to Scottee's playtext makes clear that 'within the working class there is a whole spectrum of experiences that are determined by geography, economics, cultural capital, race, ability and gender – my experience isn't *the* experience' (2020: vii) – this is much less clear in performance where the 'working class' and 'middle class' are rhetorically opposed throughout, with Scottee's specific lived experience of white, queer, urban, inner-city poverty and violence standing in as the only representation of the former.

Compounding his narrative choices, Scottee's dramaturgical aesthetic is con-structed to signal the authenticity of the lived experience he is recounting, rather than distancing the piece from it as discussed in relation to the autofictional strategies of Kene above. The real-person, non-professional aesthetic is under-pinned by props such as the photo album (see Figure 4), his intentionally naïve performance within the show of a song from his early attempt at forming a boy band and his real tears on closing the photo album which are included in the playtext as a stage direction: 'Scottee regains composure and very calm and collected wipes tears' (33). Such dramaturgical mechanisms, real or otherwise, signal a double-edged authenticity that not only serves to validate the truth of this one narrative but which might conflate, in the minds of the audience, the reality of Scottee's own story with that of the working-class subject per se, thus reducing the plurality of the working class as a whole to the culturally preferred figure of precarity.

Figure 4 Scottee as Scottee in *Class*. Photograph by Holly Revell.

Scottee is, of course, acutely aware of the danger that he and his story, as told in this way, are highly vulnerable to commodification by the industry and exotification by the audience. At one point, he asks his audience if they 'came to watch the normalised horror, to slow down at the car crash and to think "lucky me, I'm glad this didn't happen to me"' (34). Because the working-class narratives that seem to play out best on the UK stage are those that lie furthest away from the comfortable middle-class existence of those who are consuming the cultural product, as the voices of Arinzé's friends and Scottee are all aware. Scottee points out that the following evening his audience will be able to 'drink a glass of Rosé and tell each other what good people you are for coming to see this show by someone you probably wouldn't invite to a dinner party' (5). The charge of exoticisation may feel a harsh one, but the artists here, as Hurley in the previous section, are merely observing patterns in the types of working-class stories that the industry likes to stage. As noted in Sections 1 and 2, the particular left-leaning politics of the cultural fraction of the middle class are precisely what give rise to the ideological imperative for audiences to ally with the figure of precarity, in explicit opposition to those other fractions within their own class, and the wider working class, who might be expected (given the antagonisms confected by politicians and the media) to stigmatise such a figure. Thus, it might be argued, narratives of authentic precarity become required by these audiences to afford them the pleasure of offering the allyship that confirms and consolidates not only their own distance (for the most part) from precarity but also their distinctive political identity within the cultural, rather than the economic or lower-middle fractions of the middle class. That these audiences remain so often interpellated as antagonists by the precarious figures in question demonstrates the one-way direction of this allyship which, as Scottee wryly notes, is at its heart self-interested and is unlikely to include a dinner invitation for those to whom empathy is ostensibly afforded.

Scottee's complicity in this process of self-commodification is a complex operation. On the one hand, his knowing self-reflection on the audience's appetite for 'the normalised horror' of precarious or abjectified lives is designed to provoke self-recognition in the middle-class spectator (and Scottee is explicit that this play is made for such a spectator) of their own potential internalisation of the ideological imaginary of deficit. This is the strategy of subversion examined in my analysis of *Iphigenia* and *Mouthpiece*, where the repetition of tropes of abjection is undertaken by artists to expose and challenge the operation of stigmatisation in which the audience might be complicit. However, Scottee's lived experience of precarity, and his own commodification of it, he suggests, is also his ticket into the creative subset of the cultural fraction of the middle class: the attribute that gains him access to the stage, the necessary cost of participation. Like Kene's character Arinzé, Scottee reflects that this cost might be damage to himself and his own community by the very telling of his story. At the end of the first performance of *Class* I attended, in Edinburgh, there was a moment when, having challenged the audience to look in the mirror that was revealed, Scottee looked at his own reflection and questioned his own culpability: had he been exploiting the trauma of his community for his own ends?[27]

As long as exposing the trauma of one's lived experience remains the ticket to cultural access, the artist of working-class origin is compelled to continue to offer what appears to be, in the marketplace, their most valuable, commodifiable asset: their working-class-origin story, tailored to the demands of funders, producers and audiences who are inevitably, if unconsciously, caught up in the bind of the ideological imaginary of cultural and moral deficit that consigns the working-class subject to precarity, if not abjection. Kene's self-examination in *Misty* ultimately concludes, despite the subversive dramaturgical disruptions of authenticity the piece employs, that pitting the autonomy of the individual writer against the ideological implications of their work is a false premise when that autonomy itself is ideologically and commercially constrained.

So long as the ideological and aesthetic preferences of the creative subset of the subsidised theatre industry, and a dominant part of its audience, remain in the

---

[27] This moment of self-critique was not repeated in the showing at Manchester I attended, nor does it appear in the published playtext.

hands of a predominantly middle-class-origin cultural fraction, the exoticisation of the precarious figure of the working-class subject will always be a political risk, regardless of the intention of the political strategies at play explored in this, and the preceding, section. Moreover, as the next section will propose, exoticisation that is moulded into an ideological allyship between the precarious protagonist that is staged and the imagined audience figure of the cultural fraction can risk conjuring up a classed antagonist to both, who is configured out of a quite different ideological imaginary of cultural and moral deficit.

5 Allyship and Antagonism

Jez Butterworth's *Jerusalem* (2009) has arguably been one of the most success-ful and critically examined pieces of twenty-first-century new writing on the UK stage. It was first produced by the Royal Court in 2009, transferring to the Apollo Theatre in London's West End in 2010, before a sold-out and extended Broadway run in New York in 2011 and second season at the Apollo later that year. The play was again remounted at the Apollo Theatre in 2022 when I attended a performance, retaining Mark Rylance as the lead actor playing protagonist Johnny 'Rooster' Byron. *Jerusalem* has been lauded across press reviews and a swathe of scholarly criticism that will be drawn on in this section. While characterised by a diversity of theoretical perspectives, I will argue that the majority of these accounts share an implicitly classed response to the piece. An analysis of these readings productively highlights the ideological allyship demonstrated by the cultural fraction of the middle class towards the precarious outsider and, more critically, the new antagonist that can emerge in opposition to this alliance.

My own instinctive response to the performance was very much in line with the readings examined here, and both script and performance, I will argue, were designed to lead the imagined audiences of the initial Royal Court production in just such a direction. However, I am proposing that the attempt I will make in this section to place my own personal response, along with critical accounts of others, under the lens of a classed analysis, can highlight alternative readings that bring forth a new figure of cultural and moral deficit, epitomised by those living in the village of Flintock and, most critically, on its new housing estate. The existing class-focused analyses of the play (Adiseshiah, 2016; Holdsworth, 2020: 125–162; and McEvoy, 2021) share a concern that the political danger of Rooster's figuration lies in the potential exoticisation of the abjectified subject, as explored in previous sections – a tragic hero who would be vilified by that same audience were he to appear on the edge of their own lives. My own identification of the careful allegiance constructed between Rooster and the audience casts light on a second risk, which is the vilification of their common enemy: the residents of the new estate. These Butterworth portrays, through Rooster's narrative lens, as hypocritical, repressed, sexually voracious women; and hypocritical, sexually deviant and brutally violent men. The residents of the estate, I will suggest, are painted as an ambiguously classed tapestry which, nonetheless, gestures to Dan Evan's (2023) description of the 'traditional petty bourgeoisie' fraction of the lower-middle-class who are often of working-class origin. The portrayal of this class fraction as the antagonist to both Rooster and his allies in the audience, I will argue, holds the risk of exacerbating the antagonism confected in the right-wing political discourse, as detailed in Section 2, between the rhetorical figures of the 'ordinary people' of the white working and lower middle class, and the 'cultural elite'.

5.1 Ambiguity in Abjection

Rooster inhabits a dilapidated caravan in the clearing of a wood (see Figure 5). His anarchic lifestyle, drug-fuelled parties, mythological status and tales of heroic and impossible feats draw to him a motley crew of acolytes, but his Romany dwelling is an illegal one that has long fuelled anger in the local town of Flintock, a rural conurbation in the South-west of England. The play has been analysed

Figure 5 Rooster and his followers outside his caravan in the original Royal Court production. Photograph by Simon Annand.

through a number of theoretical lenses, but a key feature of the many scholarly analyses and critical reviews is the ambiguous duality of Johnny Rooster Byron, described by Julia Boll as 'both the scapegoat and the monster' (2012:1) – a figure, as Nadine Holdsworth proposes, 'to be reviled and admired in equal measure as he teeters between compelling anti-hero and repugnant waster' (2020: 148). Here, as in *Iphigenia*, we see tropes of abjection that are, as Sian Adiseshiah notes, 'overdetermined': 'Byron ... unambiguously signifies the classed position of the feckless, excessive, wanton and feral .... he is an absent father; a small-time drug dealer; sexually promiscuous; barred from the village's three pubs; a magnet for local youth; of Romany descent; and is squatting illegally on the edge of the forest' (2016: 155). The challenge to Rooster's abjectification comes via a mythological characterisation, created by Butterworth and performed by Rylance, that seeks to endow Byron with the status of a tragic anti-hero.

Although the dual figuration is acknowledged in all existing analyses of the play, the intertextual allusions and mythical tropes that construct his tragic anti-hero status overshadow any sustained attention to the more dubious aspects of his character. Anna Harpin, reading the play 'through an optic of tragedy and climate change' (2011: 63), does not shy away from the darker side of Byron, describing his figuration as 'a portrait of flawed grandeur, sexually charismatic, counter-cultural, supernatural, monstrous, with pagan, if not satanic, association' (70). However, she ultimately concludes that 'he is, then, folkloric green man – a pagan relic associated with vulgarity and drunkenness – spliced with tragic exceptionality: an extraordinary legend whose fall presages our own' (72). Harpin aligns the tragic anti-hero explicitly with the natural world, in opposition to the townspeople, the property developers, the council officials and the forces of law and order, who would all see him banished from the wood: 'for the destruction of the Rooster, read the destruction of nature and, indeed, history' (67). Holdsworth, likewise, reads *Jerusalem* as participating in a 'long-standing celebration of mythical and cultural rogues and outsiders from Robin Hood to Falstaff and Puck', characters associated with their defence of 'natural rather than judicial justice' (2020: 151). Such a defence, she observes, 'is often associated with the woods and forests of England as potentially transgressive and performative spaces' (151). Sean McEvoy also argues that 'the play's location of value in the materiality of the land of England itself is not informed by a regressive nationalist rhetoric but by a radical genealogy of legend which points forward towards the Jerusalem Blake envisioned' (2021: 122) and defines Rooster unequivocally as 'an enchanter, a scapegoat and a tragic protagonist with a distinguished literary genealogy; a Romany English hero' (122).

Byron's status as tragic anti-hero is clearly threaded through the text and production of *Jerusalem*, but what is of most interest to the analysis I am proposing here is the absence of critical attention to the less palatable aspects of Byron's character, even when these are acknowledged. Because the same mythical attributes drawn on to substantiate Byron's supernatural status can, when seen through a feminist lens, for example, be read as signals of a conventional, and dubiously virile, myth of masculinity. His own origin narrative is of a baby born from sperm attached to the tip of a bullet, teeth already present, hair on his chest, equipped with a knife and a cloak. His band of followers includes no adult females, and he boasts of the women in the town he has had sexual relationships with (33–34). Even darker is his ambiguous relationship with the young girls who party at the caravan and often sleep over in, or under, the van, albeit seemingly without his knowledge or consent. When fifteen-year-old Phaedra goes missing, her step-father, Troy, accuses Byron of hiding her, which he denies. Yet, when Phaedra later emerges from his caravan, and commands him to dance with her, there is a highly charged moment between them which is intentionally ambiguous and to which I will later return in more detail.

While many, if not most, scholarly accounts of *Jerusalem* acknowledge the tropes of abjection that form one part of the duality of Byron, these are seen predominantly as dramaturgical mechanisms that lay the ground for subversion, as Byron, regardless of his darker side, ultimately transcends his abjectified status to become a heroic, if tragic, figuration that draws on Christ's own suffering and resurrection. Yet, it remains intriguing that the potentially toxic aspects of Byron, which are precisely the building blocks on which his mythical status is built, are given so little critical weight in the wealth of academic attention the play has received. The allegiance many scholars have forged with Byron, despite his rather toxic masculinity that most would be explicitly opposed to in a different dramaturgical context, is skilfully invited by Butterworth and magnificently upheld through Rylance's powerful and deeply charismatic performance, as witnessed by myself, and noted without exception throughout reviews and academic criticism alike. Here, like Melville's performance in *Iphigenia*, we see the abjectified character redeemed through carefully crafted dialogue and the virtuosity of the actor's performance which compels the audience onto their side despite the more dubious aspects of their characterisation. Indeed, Christopher Innes goes so far as to claim that it is entirely Rylance's 'virtuoso physical acting – underlining and indeed exaggerating the significance of the body – which literally seduces the audience, destabilizing conventions and inverting standard moral responses' (2013: 78). Holdsworth, furthermore, observes how 'Byron's verbal dexterity and vibrant humour is contrasted with the council workers and their dull language of officialdom' (2020: 157), and David Ian Rabey notes how, in Rickson's production, Rylance engaged directly with the audience as if to seduce them into allegiance, imbuing

> Johnny with unfathomable moments of both distraction and power in his intermittent tendency to gaze out towards the audience . . . strangely aware of them, and implicating them, as (spirit?) witnesses (invisible to all but him) . . . as he self-consciously persisted along the dramatic and mythic stations of his own via dolorosa. (2015: 120)

The intertextual allusions to classic texts are also extensively noted in the scholarship on *Jerusalem* as a critical means of securing a mythological heroism for Byron in the mind of the spectator. For David Kerler, Byron is 'an intertextual conglomerate of numerous mythological, literary and folkloric figures, he embodies a (Romantic) sense of unity and mythic completion in face of postmodern estrangement' (2017: 73). Simon White reads him as 'an imperfect echo of the mythopoetic Blakean world-view' (2019: 259); Harpin (2011) focuses on the Byronic aspects conjured by his namesake; Graham Saunders (2017: 151–175) and Rabey (2015) engage with numerous Shakespearian reference points; McEvoy (2021) identifies Rooster as a scapegoat drawing heavily on the mythology of Christ; and Butterworth himself offers Byron an army of supernatural forces that he is able to call on to come to his aid, once his own lineage of Byrons has been exhausted:

> Rise up, Cormoran. Woden. Jack-of-Green. Jack-in-Irons. Thunderdell. Búri, Blunderbore, Gog and Magog, Galligantus, Vili and Vé, Yggdrasil, Brutus of Albion. Come, you drunken spirits. Come, you battalions. You fields of ghosts who walk these green plains still. Come, you giants! (2009: 109)

Adiseshiah argues that this is a political operation by which Rooster transcends a realistic 'type' of classed identity precisely through the numerous classical and mythical reference points that underpin his characterisation. In this way, she argues, he is able to circumvent the lens of abjectification more usually turned on those from the Romany community (2016: 155).

This reading would align the characterisation of Byron with the trickster figure highlighted in Section 3. But, unlike in *Mouthpiece* and *Iphigenia*, Butterworth's imagined audience is not placed in a strategically antagonistic relation to the abjectified protagonist in order to challenge its own prejudice but rather seduced into allegiance with him, as demonstrated in the scholarship noted in this subsection. This, then, aligns both protagonist and audience against the real villains of the play: the hapless bureaucrats, oppressive police force and, critically I will argue, the new estate. It is as much in Butterworth's construction of a common enemy who can be ideologically opposed to both Byron and the target audience, as it is in the figuration of Byron himself, that the class alliance

between the precarious Romany outsider and the imagined Royal Court spectator of the original commissioned performance is forged.

5.2 A Common Enemy

The enemies that line up against Byron consist of all those who want to evict
him from the land on which he lives, the land he claims as his wood and
birthright. The council officials who serve him notice, the townspeople, including those from the new estate, who protest his presence and sign the petition
against him, the violent would-be vigilantes who viciously attack him and the
riot police who we never see but who are on their way as the play closes. The
ideological forces that these people represent are many, but in all cases, as I will
now detail, they are ideological forces that the cultural class fraction of theatre
academics and critics are overwhelmingly likely to oppose. In his analysis of the
echoes of Shakespearian comedies in *Jerusalem*, Graham Saunders argues:
'The action to evict Byron from his home is equated with repressive forms of
puritanism because, like Malvolio's attempts to police the antics of Sir Toby and
Sir Andrew, all these fellow revellers embody a spirit of celebratory life
affirming festivity' (2017: 157). It is the health and safety concerns of the
same council who wants to evict him, Saunders further argues, that put a stop
to Byron's death-defying jumps on the trail bike, and sanitised the Flintock Fair,
which has since become 'anodyne' and commercialised (157).

   McEvoy, White, Harpin and Shaw likewise locate Byron's tragic heroism in
his resistance to wider – and hegemonic – neoliberal forces which prioritise
rationalism over enchantment, capitalist organisation over nature's rhythms,
capitalist growth over ecological survival. McEvoy sees in the forces ranged
against Byron 'the dangers a community faces from an instrumental rationalism
the consequences of whose destructive and dehumanising power have now
become all too urgent' (2021: 122). White notes that the townspeople's 'dislike
of his messy (in both the physical and the legal sense of the word) occupation of
a marginal place on the edge of the community . . . is rooted in an unconscious
and unmitigated adherence to the rationalist-capitalist view of the land as
a resource to be organised for the benefit of humankind' (2019: 269). Harpin
concludes that 'by tracing the logic of the mythical and poetic allusions here,
one can discern a clear sense that the attack on Rooster Byron is simultaneously
an attack on the land' (2011: 67), while Katy Shaw highlights how 'Johnny
represents the loss of the local, of alternative narratives, other ways of being, the
home-grown and the ancient as set against the corporate and commercialized'
(2018: 55). Byron's opposition to the neoliberal, the rational, the corporate and
the commercialised will align him with the political preferences of a Royal

Court audience and theatre academics and reviewers made up predominantly of the cultural fraction of the middle class, as discussed in Section 2 of this Element, but above all it is the ideological positioning of the townspeople as sedentary that forges the most secure alliance between the Romany figure of travel and the cosmopolitan ethos of that cultural fraction.

In her detailed analysis of Byron's Romany identity, Holdsworth discusses how 'cultural imaginaries have played a part in fetishising and sedimenting a view of Gypsy and Traveller communities as either romantic outsiders or out of control, uncivilised, amoral and above all in need of control and containment' (2020: 126). For the townspeople of Flintock, Byron is perceived through the latter lens and Holdsworth draws on Tim Cresswell's (2006) work on 'sedentarist metaphysics' to describe the predominant ideological imaginary of the townspeople as 'a mode of being and thinking that values notions of territory, roots and boundedness' (Holdsworth 2020: 128). Consequently, as Cresswell argues, Gypsies and Travellers are people negatively cast 'as figures of mobile threat in need of straightening out and discipline' (Cresswell, 2006: 26 in Holdsworth, 2020: 128). Citing Imogen Tyler, Holdsworth further notes that 'no wonder then that Gypsies and Travellers "whose entire history has been one of struggle *against* capitalist systems of wage-labour entrapment" are viewed with suspicion as nomadism is perceived as a threat to the ideological principles that underpin sedentarism itself' (Tyler, 2013: 142 (original emphasis) in Holdsworth, 2020: 129).

The anti-sedentarism of the Romany may ignite the anger of the townspeople trapped in their ideological imaginary of sedentarism, but this same mobility and resistance to social conventional norms is precisely what gives rise to the 'romantic outsider' figuration that allies the cultural fraction of the middle class on the side of Byron against the townspeople. As Holdsworth notes, characters like Byron are attractive to certain theatre audiences because they 'resonate with a deep-rooted appetite for anti-establishment behaviour, especially in the safe space of the theatrical mode' (2020: 158). In romanticised, if not material, terms, Holdsworth suggests, there is a shared territory, rather than an antagonism, between the Romany traveller and the anticipated Royal Court spectators, who would also want to resist the sedentarism imposed by 'capitalist systems of wage-labour entrapment' as noted by Tyler above.[28]

---

[28] An even more unexpected inter-class allegiance with Rooster is suggested by Gemma Edwards (2021), who draws lines of connection between the ancestral bloodlines of the aristocrat and those of Rooster; their affinity to related, if distinct, versions of a historic myth of Deep England; and their antipathy to the encroachment of the new housing estate which appals, and critically threatens, the rural visions of aristocrat and Romany alike.

5.3 Beyond the Royal Court Audience

Jerusalem and the crafting of Byron in script and performance exemplify a dramaturgy that aligns the precarious outsider with the anticipated Royal Court spectator's world view, despite the significant character failings as noted above. Yet, this ideal spectator is not the only spectator to attend *Jerusalem,* even if the published critical accounts of the play are inevitably offering readings from the perspective of that same class fraction. *Jerusalem's* outstanding success, with multiple runs in the West End and Broadway, has ensured that a much wider audience than that originally anticipated (albeit still somewhat curtailed by high ticket prices and the speed in which the shows sold out) has encountered the show who might reject the inter-class alliance that Butterworth seeks.

David Ian Rabey recounts how George Monbiot reflected that 'though it is now almost universally admired, when Jez Butterworth's play *Jerusalem* began to be noticed it sharply divided its audience. At the end of the performance I watched, in the last week of its first, incandescent West End run, half the audience stood to applaud, the rest barged out with thunderous faces, snapping and muttering' (Monbiot, 2013: 47 in Rabey, 2015: 133). Rabey adds his own memory of overhearing 'one expression of distaste that Butterworth should appear to present a "criminal and drug dealer as some sort of Christ figure"' (2015: 133). Yet readings such as these, which rejected the heroic, or tragic, narrative outlined above, are scarce, if not absent, from the substantial body of academic criticism which has been written about the show. It is significant that, as Monbiot notes, such responses were evident in the first West End run, before the critical acclaim of the cultural fraction had fully established what the authorised response should be.

This is important because, as Katie Beswick argues, while there is significant evidence pertaining to the dominance of the middle class in the make-up of (especially subsidised) theatre audiences, this is not to say that working class spectators do not exist, but that the ones that do, are to some extent 'invisible' (2019: 80): their perspectives too often occluded by the creative class in whose hands the critical receptions most often lie. This matters, as Beswick argues, 'because representations may be understood differently by different audience members depending on their upbringing, life experiences and relationship to the material on stage .... because habitus structures how we understand the world' (80). By attempting to suspend my own response to the piece, and reading against the seductions (although not the details) of Byron's characterisation, I now aim to offer an alternatively classed reading of *Jerusalem,* which might not only lead the future spectator to hesitate before accepting the play's invitation to hold allegiance with Byron, but to consider more critically the antagonism they are encouraged to forge with his enemies.

5.4 Ambiguously Classed Subjects

Byron's classed identity, as a precarious Romany outsider, is clear in the play and consistent in the critical literature analysing *Jerusalem*, but the class fractions to which his followers and the townspeople who oppose his presence belong, are understood less consistently, reflecting the greater ambiguity with which these are presented in the text and performance. His followers are commonly located somewhere between those fractions of the working class in low-paid employment and the fraction I have categorised as the precariat, who sit in the very lowest economic fraction of the working class and are most commonly stigmatised as abject in mainstream representation. Saunders refers to Byron's own classification of them as 'Outcasts! Leeches! Undesirables!' (Butterworth, 2009: 50). Likewise, for McEvoy, they are working-class characters who, within this broader category, are 'precarious' in their economic situation and 'marginal' in their social status (2021: 136). Other accounts, such as those by Harpin (2011) and Adiseshiah (2016) emphasise that they are, nonetheless, for the most part, characterised by their labour, rather than an absence of employment, 'who, in their roles as plasterers, decorators and abattoir workers, and in their gleeful humour, recall Bottom and his mechanicals' (Harpin, 2011: 69). Economist Paul Mason further argues that they exemplify

> the life of a poor- ish, prospectless, rave- addicted, casual drug using, unskilled social group that is absolutely central to the society we live in, but which the media barely notices exists. [...] The West End theatre reviewers tended to describe this demographic as a 'bucolic underclass', 'wastrels', 'waifs and strays'. But the power of the play lies in the fact that Rooster's [...] outcasts are not at all marginal to real life in Britain. (Mason, 2009 in Rabey, 2015:134)

If Byron and his disciples are read as examples of the broader working class, in the way that Mason, Harpin and Adiseshiah suggest, then the antagonism between them and the townspeople is more easily read as straightforward class antagonism, with the new estate, in particular, providing the middle-class, economically aspirant, conformist opposition. This is certainly Adiseshiah's reading of the piece, which notes that the piece avoids becoming a piece of 'prole porn' (2016: 158), an exoticised working-class Romany theatricalised for a middle-class audience, precisely through the recognition of the audience of their class alignment to those who commit horrific violence on Byron. This, she persuasively argues, makes visible 'the violence of classed ways of knowing' (158), and thus offers the audience a point of self-critical identification that provides the political heft of the production, much the same operation I identified in *Mouthpiece*. Yet, in *Mouthpiece*, the antagonist, Libby, in her role as playwright, belonged to the same cultural fraction of the middle class as the intended audience for the piece. This enabled Hurley to invite the audience to consider their own acts of class violence, committed through an aesthetic exploitation of the dispossessed as modelled by Libby. Conversely, in *Jerusalem*, those living in the town, and on the new estate, as will be examined below, are the ideological antithesis of the intended spectator, and so the operation of self-reflection is somewhat compromised and, I will now argue, might even serve to consolidate existing, intra-class antagonism.

Although it is the council officials and the police who are the state-sanctioned arm of the violent eviction of Byron from his home, and the people of Flintock, as a whole, who campaign for such an eviction, the enemy of everything that Byron stands for is most clearly represented by the new estate which, as Holdsworth proposes, can be read as 'the epitome of neoliberal sedentarism' (2020: 153). It is the new estate that features on Rooster's protest banner (see Figure 5), it is from here that the violence of Troy[29] and his friends erupts, here that the attraction of a further new estate to be built by property developers on Byron's land originates and, critically, here that the most sustained opposition to Byron's presence is bolstered through the residents' significant contributions to town hall meetings and petitions. While residents of the new estate are presented as holding greater economic heft than Byron and his followers, by virtue of their propertied status, their class status is far from unambiguously middle class or necessarily comfortably affluent. As Davey states, these are properties that 'you've sweat your bollocks off to buy' (2009: 30), suggesting that these are unlikely to be cash buyers or second homes, but at the very top of the limit that their residents can afford. Furthermore, as Saunders comments in a footnote, 'contrary to widely reported stories of locals being priced out of property by city dwellers, in *Jerusalem*, it appears that the majority living on the new estate are locals' (2017: 173). Troy and his friends grew up in the town, they visited Byron when they were young, and this suggests a sedentarism, a rootedness in place which, especially in a rural locality, would be more common among working-class-origin communities than the households of the typical Royal Court spectator, as the cultural fraction of the middle class, indeed the professional-managerial middle class more broadly, tends to be much more geographically mobile (Evans, 2023: 252–253). Nonetheless, it remains

---

[29] Although only the character of Pea, one of the young girls who frequents Rooster's caravan, is explicitly identified as a resident of the new estate, the logic of the play suggests that her friend Phoebe, Phoebe's stepfather Troy and Troy's friends are from that same community which is foregrounded throughout as Rooster's greatest enemy.

difficult to confidently assert that the residents of the new estate are working class, as Shaw identifies them (2018: 52), given Davey's description of at least one type of property as 'Detached house, three beds with garden overlooking wood' (2009: 30).

Such contra-indications suggest that the class demography of the new estate might be best defined by Julia Boll's description of 'an overlooked part of the population, the disillusioned lower middle class, deprived of its individuality and pride, void of a distinctive identity' (2012: 7). This is the liminal class fraction identified by Dan Evans as the traditional 'petty bourgeoisie', composed of small employers and self-employed own account workers, often of working-class origin and without university-level education. Evans draws on Duncan Weldon's *Barrett Britain* to propose that new-build estates are predominantly occupied by the more affluent among this class fraction and, significantly for my argument here, are sharply divided from the cultural fraction of the middle class by their chosen habitus, arguing that 'class divides are expressed, understood and lived through housing aesthetics ... new-build versus tasteful Victorian terrace, AstroTurf garden with faux olive trees versus bohemian rewilded garden to help the bees' (265).

The cultural fraction of the middle class are characterised by their preference for the second of each of the binaries that Evans sets up, and the typical Royal Court spectator would, resources permitting, be far more likely to inhabit characterful cottages from the original village than be a resident on the new estate. Those less economically affluent within this class fraction might well, like the Professor, be more at home sitting around the caravan with Byron. Regardless of income, the cultural habitus of this class fraction, despite the political support on the left for new homes to be built in the UK, is one in which the idea of new builds remains aesthetically jarring. Evans identifies the social media discourse which suggests that the identikit nature of new-build estates, their lack of history and individual features and even the neatness of their gardens, all offer a lack of cultural distinction that, *pace* Bourdieu, is unattractive to bohemian taste which, to some degree or other, tends to characterise the housing preferences of the cultural fraction of the middle class. As Evans notes, the professional-managerial class on the left understand the need for housing very well, but that does not stem the class snobbery that underpins the popularity of social media threads such as 'newbuild hate' (2023: 267).

Identifying the habitus of the new estate as that of the lower middle class offers alternative readings of class antagonisms to those identified by Adiseshiah (2016). The habitus of the new estate now invites consideration not of an *inter*-class antagonism between working class (Byron and his followers) and middle class (audience and new estate) but rather of three possibilities of *intra*-class antagonism. The first opposes the more precarious fraction of the working class (Byron and his followers) with the more affluent working-class-origin and/or lower-middle-class inhabitants of the new estate. This would mirror the political discourse outlined in Section 2, in which the rhetorical figure of 'hard-working families', composed of the affluent working and lower middle classes, is hailed as the enemy of a precarious underclass which threatens the terms of their existence. The second is the antagonism that those on the new estate display towards Rooster because of his Romany origin, mirroring the right-wing political discourse that pits 'ordinary people' against racialised outsiders. The third is the antagonism that consequently ensues between the cultural fraction of the middle class in the audience and the working-class-origin/lower-middle-class inhabitants of the new estate. The allyship of the audience for the precarious protagonist makes the new estate the common enemy of both. As detailed in Section 2, this allyship, especially when given to a racialised outsider, can be weaponised in right-wing discourse to construct the populist figure of the (implicitly white) 'ordinary people' and set it against the equally rhetorical figure of the 'cultural elite'. The vilification of the new estate can thus raise the spectre of a new ideological imaginary of cultural and moral deficit, where the white working-class-origin and lower-middle-class figure,[30] becomes synonymous with bad taste, complicity with consumerism and racist violence.

5.5 Shifting Perspective

The new estate is portrayed at its most deplorable and indefensible through the violent attack on Byron by Troy and his henchmen, who come looking for Troy's stepdaughter Phaedra who has gone missing. While neither Troy's suspicions that Rooster is knowingly harbouring his fifteen-year-old nor Rooster's counter-accusation that Troy himself holds sexual desire for her are proven either way, the dramaturgy of the narrative and staging ensure that the spectator's sympathy will align with Rooster, the brutality of the violence playing no little part in an instinctive repugnance for Troy and his friends, and an empathy for their victim. Holdsworth cites Troy's 'sexually loaded verbal assault' (2020: 155) on sixteen–year-old Pea, as evidence of his brutality and misogyny: 'Just fucking open your cockhole one more time, I'll shut if for good. Shut the fuck up. You wanna say some more? Little bitch. Little cocksucker' (Butterworth, 2009: 80). McEvoy

---

[30] In the 2022 production I attended, there were actors of colour among the young girls from the new estate visiting Rooster, but from the images of the original Royal Court production, these characters appeared to be played by white actors. The inclusion of actors of colour in later productions would be in line with the changes in racial politics of casting following the BLM movement in 2020, but the original casting suggests that Butterworth/Rickson imagined the new estate residents as predominantly white.

draws attention to the strong semiotic signals of the attack that likewise suggest that Rooster is the knight and Troy is the dragon:

> One of his [Troy's] men *'has a blowtorch and a branding iron'*. But this fire-breathing monster will not be slain by this St George, the protector of the damsel in distress. Johnny is a tragic St George. In response to the fiery attack Johnny *'stretches his arms wide, smiling'* before he is overpowered. The allusion to the gesture of crucifixion is reinforced by the crosses branded onto both his cheeks by his assailant, as he stumbles out of the caravan after the beating, mutilated and bleeding. (McEvoy, 2021: 137)

Yet, despite the strength of such readings, which very much reflected my own response at the production, there is more ambiguity in the confrontation between Rooster and Troy than most critics seem keen to acknowledge. This ambiguity derives from two things: firstly, despite Troy's hate-filled, misogynistic language, there is no evidence other than Rooster's own accusation that he has an unhealthy relationship with his step-daughter. Conversely, Rooster's own close relationships with girls on the margin of the age of consent are not so easily discounted, and his encounter with Phaedra held a distinctly sexual charge on the night that I saw the production, when they danced together and embraced (see Figure 6). 'I seen you looking at me', Phaedra says to him, 'You like me just fine'. To which Rooster responds, 'You should watch yourself. You should get yourself away lass' (Butterworth, 2009: 103). McEvoy is among those who hold that 'there is nothing to confirm that Johnny has had sex with her; in fact he warns her off' (2021: 127). Yet, even were this true, it does not make him innocent. My own reading of the moment was that Johnny's warning to Phaedra arose precisely from his own desire for her: it was himself he was warning her against. The stage directions also suggest something more might well have happened if Troy and his friends hadn't arrived at just that point:

> *She puts on music. She starts to dance. She takes his hand, he stands up. They dance together.*
> *They stop, looking into each other's eyes. Close. Suddenly she turns and flees.*
> (104)

Yet, this alternative reading of Rooster, even if only hinted at, sits awkwardly with the dominant readings of his tragic anti-hero status, and so is generally either discredited or ignored. Sean Carney, for example, chooses to read the embrace metaphorically, with Byron figured as

> a weary and beleaguered knight and Phaedra as his fearsome Queen in the midst of an enchanted forest that is now passing from the mortal world. The

Figure 6 Rooster and Phoebe embrace. Photograph by Simon Annand.

desperate, heartfelt, and prolonged embrace between Byron and Phaedra . . .
communicated the subtext of the moment clearly: Byron's desire to protect
her from her brute reality, to stop time and maintain her youth, and the futility
of these desires were all evoked by the embrace. (2013: 296)

Many readings are possible, and the counter-hegemonic analysis that I offer
here is not claiming to over-ride alternative accounts or, indeed, my own
response to the play in performance. But what it highlights is the degree to
which the dominant readings of Rooster as tragic anti-hero are arrived at
through a lens that might be described as 'classed': through an allegiance of
cultural professionals and their intended audiences with the precarious outsider,
forged, despite a toxic masculinity and hints of possible paedophilia, through
a shared ideological and classed antagonism to the neoliberal sedentarism,
material aspiration and social conformity which characterises, and arguably
stigmatises, the residents of the new estate. Troy, of course, is the unquestion-
able, and irredeemable, villain of the play, but his hate-filled racist and misogynistic language and the brutal violence he inflicts on Rooster emerge, in
Butterworth's narrative, from a class of people who are given few redeeming
features, and who share Troy's ultimate objectives, if not his methods. What
does indeed operate as subversive class politics, by enabling the protagonist,
Rooster, to transcend stigmatising representations of the abjectified subject

through mythological intertextuality, anti-neoliberal political resistance and charismatic performance, might also be operating as a mechanism that redirects the ideological imaginary of cultural and moral deficit away from the abjectified subject and towards other fractions of the (implicitly white) aspirant working, or lower middle classes who are figured here, at best, as hypocritical and intolerant and, at worst, as violent, sexist and racist. Such a redirection risks strengthening, not challenging, the class antagonisms between 'ordinary people' and the 'cultural elite' that are stoked by the hard-right to further a nationalist populism, as detailed in Section 2.

6 Making Theatre by Making Shoes (and Other Things) Together

6.1 *12 Last Songs*

The first iteration of Quarantine Theatre's *12 Last Songs* was staged at Leeds Playhouse on Saturday, 23 October 2021, from twelve noon until twelve midnight.[31] The durational performance consisted of around thirty people occupying the stage at different times, demonstrating their particular job while responding spontaneously to a series of projected questions put to them by the host performers. It might seem counter-intuitive, for an Element that has focused on class divisions and conflict, to conclude with a project that explicitly stages acts of labour from across the socio-economic classification spectrum (including labour that would not be recognised as such in the economic schema) in such a way that eradicates, to a great degree, class and status distinction altogether. But, by so doing, I want to propose that an alternative way of challenging the multiple ideological imaginaries of cultural and moral deficit identified throughout this Element might be for theatre to turn away from classed representations altogether, and explore, instead, the political potential of prefiguring a different way of perceiving the intersections between labour and identity, with a thoughtfulness as to where class distinctions might be productively suspended, rather than interrogated or ideologically weaponised. In *12 Last Songs*, I will argue, the rhetorical descriptors of 'left behind', 'hard-working families', 'ordinary people' and 'elites' that have featured in this Element as terms of division have no role to play in an inclusive, egalitarian (and no longer classed) category of working people that encompasses workers from all class fractions, including those from the cultural fraction of the middle class, and the artists and technicians whose current labour is that of producing the event as it unfolds. This equalising move echoes Nicholas Ridout's (2013) call for a theatrical communism, both in

---

[31] It has subsequently been produced in Brighton, Manchester, Strasbourg, Cambridge, Reykjavic and Glasgow.

the sense that Ridout's study is exploring, where the analysis addresses the labour inherent to the act of theatre itself, but also in its prefiguring of a type of theatrical communism of its own.

On the stage before us, I watched a portrait painter sketching naked life models, a stage technician, a hairdresser, a plumber, a decorator, a nursery nurse, a lecturer in midwifery, a dog groomer, an opera singer and many more, all undertaking their own everyday occupation alongside other workers. In some instances, this act of labour was both representational (by nature of being framed for an audience) and simultaneously 'real' in the sense that its original purpose was maintained and carried out (a woman had her braids plaited over three hours, a dog was groomed) (see Figure 7). In others, the act of labour was a demonstration (albeit that a wall still got papered, something was drilled) for the purposes of performance only. Alongside these workers working, the theatre workers, the hosts of the performance, also worked, greeting the workers as they arrived, asking them a series of questions from the 670 questions that ran in total throughout the day, introducing the show and the workers to audience members who came and went throughout the durational performance. So, in a very straightforward sense, workers and occupations were equalised in this production;[32] each simply got on with their particular job in hand, and the totality of the jobs in hand made up the performance event. A stage was created here for workers working alongside other workers that would not cross paths in the world beyond the theatre: here, occupations were spatialised horizontally, and enabled to co-exist and inter-cut with each other, rather than organised in the compartmentalised and hierarchical verticality of class.

This prefiguration of egalitarianism underpins my proposal that something akin to Ridout's theatrical communism was at work here, given the production did indeed seek to 'unsettle our capacity to distinguish between work and nonwork, poesis and praxis, the professional and the amateur'; an operation, as Ridout confirms, that 'will always . . . have something to do with a critique of the division of labour within capitalism' (2013: 17). Where *12 Last Songs* seems at first to depart from Ridout's theoretical framework is in a dramaturgy that, at first analytical glance, ensures that each performer is to be explicitly, and solely, identified by their 'place in the organization of labour' (2013: 18). Ridout rather suggests, *pace* Rancière, that the act of politics required for theatrical communism would be an 'undoing of the terms by which identity is conferred upon a subject by the work that they do' (18). However, each performer in *12 Last Songs* is precisely not 'placed' in a hierarchy, nor are

---

[32] Every worker was paid the same hourly rate for their participation in the production.

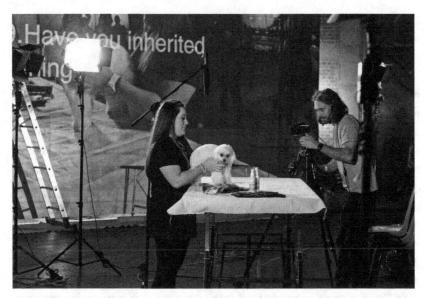

Figure 7 Hailey Watson grooms Luna the Dog. Photograph by Simon Banham.

they solely framed by their act of labour, but individualised by the questions asked of them throughout the duration of their time on stage: questions that are not designed to 'fit' any particular occupation or social background, but which cut across any classed (or other) expectations, enabling the spontaneous responses of the performers to determine equivalent, yet individual, human subjects, who are thus dis-aligned from the extra-theatrical labour task which they are concurrently undertaking.

6.2 Theatres of Real People

12 Last Songs would be defined as a 'theatre of real people', under the rubric proposed by Ulrike Garde and Meg Mumford (2016), but its political charge was shaped by its very resistance to the idea of the 'unfamiliar' which underpins Garde and Mumford's analysis of the political currency of the dramaturgical model more widely. Drawing on the work undertaken by Matthias Lilienthal at Berlin's Hebbel am Ufer theatre, Garde and Mumford argue that

> A significant contributor to a sense of the unfamiliar in the productions we explore is the staging of people who may be perceived by those involved as different, foreign or insufficiently known. This is because of, first, their occupational, socio-economic, and ethnic background, and second, their status as 'theatre strangers' – that is, as non-professional performers who do not usually perform their everyday activities in the theatre and thus represent a kind of 'foreign body' (Roselt, 2006: 34) on stage. (2016: 90)

In *12 Last Songs* the majority of the performers were certainly 'theatre strangers', or what performance company Rimini Protokoll have termed 'experts of the everyday'. However, they were not intended to be unfamiliar to those spectating through 'social-class differences' that marked them as 'unfamiliar' to the anticipated audience (90). The class (and race) composition of the intended audiences for Lilienthal's work is not explicitly highlighted by Garde and Mumford, but from the descriptions of those who might be 'unfamiliar' to the audience, it would appear, in Germany as in the UK, to be anticipated to be predominantly middle class and white. Because the 'real' people who populate the productions that feature throughout their study, as well as being most often people of colour, are mostly required to work in precarious occupations[33] and/or to inhabit the poorer neighbourhoods of the city, such as the district of Neukölln where Lilianthal's *X-Apartments* took place, known to the anticipated audiences, 'only in the form of prejudices' (Garde and Mumford, 2016: 140).

Conversely, *12 Last Songs* does not seek to present class 'strangers' to their audience, imbued with all the problematic risks of exoticisation and voyeurism this Element has identified in such an operation, but rather to construct a theatrical community in which diversity is not a mis-named and arguably singular 'otherness' to an implicit and unspoken norm, but a plurality of differences that are treated as nonetheless equivalent across class boundaries on and offstage, and between stage and auditorium. The durational aspect of the performance helped to blur boundaries between those on and off the stage: performers and spectators alike came and went throughout the day; spectators played the part allocated to them by the performance, just as those performing did, and the final questions of the evening were addressed to them to contemplate. There was no sense that those we were watching were classed, or configured, in a way that was any different from the diversity of the audience who attended. Given Quarantine's reputation, there were those in the Leeds audience who, like myself and my friend, were 'theatre professionals'; but there were also those in the audience who were self-evidently (given the many greetings and acknowledgements) friends or family of the performers and so, like the performers themselves, hailed from the numerous and diverse communities that make up the city in question, invited to convivially co-exist in order to share space and personal reflections for this one day.

---

[33] Such as Rimini Protokoll's *Call Cutta; Mobile Phone Theatre*, featuring Indian call-centre workers, and *Mr Dağacar and the Golden Tectonics of Trash*, featuring rubbish-recyclers in Istanbul.

6.3 Looking Ahead

This is not to suggest that any model of theatre can deliver an egalitarian utopia, the very real material inequalities in the city of Leeds beyond the theatre will not be changed by anything that occurs in *12 Last Songs*, and the flattening of class differentiation might, in a different reading of the show, risk proposing an equality within the cultural space of the performance that papers over the reality beyond it. For me, however, the production's value was in its prefiguration of how a world without the hierarchies of value attribution to specific acts of labour might affectively feel. In one memorable moment of the performance, an Imam, an MP and an artist/ex-drug dealer chatted convivially around a table in response to questions such as 'have you ever been arrested?' and 'do you vote?', while two members of the army, identified by their t-shirts also as Event Staff, inflated a giant slide. Subsequently, with the question 'is the world how you imagined?' in the background, the three men joyfully and repeatedly climb up and slide down the giant inflatable one after the other to audience applause. A woman later confesses that this had made her cry with happiness. *12 Last Songs* is, perhaps, a microcosm of the 'convivial multiculture', proposed by Sivamohan Valluvan, that 'becomes empirically distinctive only because it is always existing contiguously to the multiple divisions that are routinely framed by race and ethnicity' (2019: 205) and, I would add, by class. Such divisions, I would suggest, *pace* Valluvan, are so insistently highlighted in public and political discourse that they continue to press themselves upon the spectator's awareness even as the performance itself pushes them aside, and it is this very tension between existing social relations of conflict and the 'conviviality' that is shown here as possible that gives the performance its political weight.

12 Last Songs did not stage class conflict in the ways that this Element has predominantly examined, but might rather be read, in its rejection of all hierarchical classification of labour, as a fight against classification per se. The danger with class descriptors, as Tyler argues, citing Waterton, is that they are 'not only descriptive of the world, they have consequences in the world and are "operative" – defining the possibilities for action and bounding one's sense of agency' (Waterton, 2003: 113 in Tyler, 2015: 502). Declassification, Tyler argues, rather seeks the 'development of alternative social and political imaginaries, since a genuinely alternative society will require a radical openness to new forms of class alliance against neoliberalism' (2015: 508). *12 Last Songs* may, or may not, have been designed with this political aim in mind, but its prefiguration of a world in which class divisions and hierarchies had been temporarily suspended encouraged reflection on the kind of community that could be forged in their absence.

It has become apparent, through the research undertaken for this Element, that theatre and scholarship (including my own) that seeks to challenge the multiple ideological imaginaries of working-class deficit that circulate in the contemporary political and social landscape of the UK, through an analysis of named classed figures and conflicts, is simultaneously playing its part in consolidating the authority of hierarchical systems of value, even as it seeks to overturn them. I would still hold that there is political value in this: if things are not able to be measured and identified, they are not able to be exposed or challenged, but the side effects of such political operations need to be acknowledged and, where possible, mitigated. Because as long as the subsidised theatre sector (and those writing about it) remains socially and ideologically closed, and so long as its audiences remain predominantly from a single class fraction, the intentions of the political operations mounted in this shared habitus to unsettle classed assumptions and preju-dices will be derailed in one way or another by the fact that the material and cultural hierarchies of value, both aesthetic and political, remain undis-turbed. This Element hopes to have exposed just some of those possible derailments in highlighting how attempts to subvert the stigmatisation of the precarious subject, in allyship with the precariat, can lead, firstly, to a reduction in the diversity of working-class figures explored and, secondly, to two unforeseen manifestations of the ideological imaginary of working-class deficit. Firstly, the working-class-origin artist, whose cultural value risks becoming, precisely, their origin story of precarity, if not abjection; secondly, the white working- or lower-middle-class subject conjured from the ideological imaginary of the rhetorical figure of 'ordinary people' to be figured as racist and intolerant.

On 4 July 2024, a new Labour government began its term in office, having won back the votes of the majority of ex-Labour working-class constituencies they lost to the Conservatives in 2019. Yet, Nigel Farage's Reform UK gained 14.3 per cent of the vote share and now have five Members of Parliament, the far right continues to grow their parliamentary share in countries across Europe, and Donald Trump is re-elected in the United States. To return, in conclusion, to the political analysis of class that set the scene for this Element, an address to the cultural fraction of the middle-class to reject the populist narrative that fosters the latest ideo-logical imaginary in which the 'ordinary' (implicitly white) working- and lower-middle-classes are figured as irredeemably racist becomes increas-ingly critical. Now might well be the time for artists to relieve their audiences from accusations of complicity with a stigmatisation that, given their dominant class fraction, they are unlikely to accept or own.

More urgent, perhaps, than the consolidation of an existing ideological allyship between the precariat and the cultural fraction of the middle class might be a consideration as to how dramaturgical operations of solidarity and declassification might enable people of different class, and racial, backgrounds to meet in a 'convivial multiculture' on the theatrical and political stage, to exchange different answers to difficult questions, before climbing up, and flying down, the inflatable slide together.

References

Adiseshiah, S. (2016). '"Chavs", "Gyppos" and "Scum"? Class in Twenty-First -Century Drama'. Adiseshiah, S., and LePage, L. (eds.) *Twenty-First Century Drama: What Happens Now*. London: Palgrave Macmillan.

Angelaki, V. (2017). *Social and Political Theatre in 21st-Century Britain: Staging Crisis*. London: Bloomsbury Methuen.

Bartley, S. (2020). *Performing Welfare: Applied Theatre, Unemployment, and Participation*. Basingstoke: Palgrave Macmillan.

Beswick, K. (2019). *Social Housing in Performance: The English Council Estate on and off Stage*. London: Methuen.

Beswick, K. (2020). 'Feeling Working Class: Affective Class Identification and Its Implications for Overcoming Inequality'. *Studies in Theatre and Performance* 40:3, pp. 265–274. http://doi.org/10.1080/14682761.2020.1807194.

Boll, J. (2012). 'The Sacred Dragon in the Woods: On Jez Butterworth's *Jerusalem*'. *FORUM: University of Edinburgh Postgraduate Journal of Culture & The Arts* 14. https://doi.org/10.2218/forum.14.633.

Bottero, W. (2004). 'Class Identities and the Identity of Class'. *Sociology* 38:5, pp. 985–1003. http://doi:10.1177/0038038504047182.

Bourdieu, P. (2010). *Distinction: A Social Critique of the Judgement of Taste*, 4th ed. Translated by Nice R., Abingdon: Routledge.

Brennan, H. (2021). 'Tax Rises "Not Sustainable" for Hard-Working Families'. *Daily Telegraph*, 8 October 2021. (telegraph.co.uk).

Brook, O., O'Brien, D., Taylor, M. (2020). *Culture Is Bad for You*. Manchester: Manchester University Press.

Bush, C. (2021). *Hungry*. Nick Herne Books.

Butler, J. (2015). *Notes toward a Performance Theory of Assembly*. Cambridge, MA: Harvard University Press.

Butterworth, J. (2009). *Jerusalem*. London: Nick Herne Books.

Carney, S. (2013). *The Politics and Poetics of Contemporary English Tragedy*. Toronto: University of Toronto Press.

Clark, A. (2018). 'Drawn from Life: Why Have Novelists Stopped Making Things Up?' *Guardian*, 23 June 2018. www.theguardian.com/books/2018/jun/23/drawn-from-life-why-have-novelistsstopped-making-things-up.

Cresswell, T. (2006). *On the Move: Mobility in the Modern Western World*. New York: Routledge.

Deacon, M. (2023). 'Trigger Warnings Are Now Everywhere – the Cultural Elite Must Think Us Stupid'. *Telegraph*, 6 July 2023. (telegraph.co.uk).

Denham, A. (2024). 'Labour Is about to Give Middle England a Simple Choice: Emigrate or Give Up'. *Daily Telegraph*, 13 June 2024. (telegraph.co.uk).

Edwards, G. (2021). 'This Is England 2021: Staging England and Englishness in Contemporary Theatre'. *JCDE* 9:2, pp. 281–303. https://doi.org/10.1515/jcde-2021-0024.

Ellis, C. (2022). 'A Narrowing of the British Conservative Mind?' *Society* 59 pp. 682–690.

Evans, D. (2023). *A Nation of Shopkeepers: The Unstoppable Rise of the Petty Bourgeoisie*. London: Repeater Books.

Evans, G., Tilley, J. (2017). *The New Politics of Class: The Political Exclusion of the British Working Class*. Oxford: Oxford University Press.

Florida, R. (2002). *The Rise of the Creative Class*. New York: Basic Books.

Fragkou, M. (2018). *Ecologies of Precarity in Twenty-First Century Theatre: Politics, Affect, Responsibility*. London: Bloomsbury Methuen.

Friedman, S., O'Brien, D., Laurison, D. (2017). '"Like Skydiving without a Parachute": How Class Origin Shapes Occupational Trajectories in British Acting'. *Sociology* 51:5, pp. 992–1010. https://doi.org/10.1177/0038038516629917.

Garde, U., Mumford, M. (2016). *Theatre of Real People: Diverse Encounters at Berlin's Hebbel am Ufer and Beyond*. London: Bloomsbury Methuen.

Goddard, L. (2015). *Contemporary Black British Playwrights: Margins to Mainstream*. London: Palgrave Macmillan.

Goodhart, D. (2017). *The Road to Somewhere: The New Tribes Shaping British Politics*. London: Penguin Books.

Gualberto, R. (2021). 'Adaptation against Myth: Gary Owen's Iphigenia in Splott and the Violence of Austerity'. *Alicante Journal of English Studies* 35, pp. 119–140.

Harpin, A. (2011). 'Land of Hope and Glory: Jez Butterworth's Tragic Landscapes'. *Studies in Theatre and Performance* 31:1, pp. 61–73. https://doi.org/10.1386/stap.31.1.61_1.

Hescott, T., Furness, C. (2018). *The Director's Voice: A Study of Theatre Director Training and Career Development in the UK*. https://stagedirectorsuk.com/wp-content/uploads/2019/01/DirectorsVoiceDec2018.pdf.

Holdsworth, N. (2020). *English Theatre and Social Abjection: A Divided Nation*. Basingstoke: Palgrave Macmillan.

Howe, D. (2003). ' Fallout review'. *New Statesman*. 30 June 2003. Reprinted in *Theatre Record* 23(11–12) (21 May–17 June 2003), 760.

Hughes, J. (2015). 'The Theatre and Its Poor: Neoliberal Economies of Waste and Gold in *Les Misérables* (1985) and *Road* (1986)'. *Theatre Journal* 67, pp. 1–19.

Hurley, K. (2018). *Mouthpiece*. London: Oberon Modern Plays.

Innes, C. (2013). 'Triumphant Physical Theatre: Undermining Ethics through the Body'. *JCDE* 1:1, pp. 70–79.

Jannarone, K. (ed.) (2015). *Vanguard Performance beyond Left and Right*. Ann Arbor: University of Michigan Press.

Jarness, V., Flemmen, M. P., Rosenlund, L. (2019). 'From Class Politics to Classed Politics'. *Sociology* 53:5, pp. 879–899.

Jeffers, A. (2012). *Refugees, Theatre and Crisis: Performing Global Identities*. Basingstoke: Palgrave Macmillan.

Jones, O. (2016). *Chavs: The Demonization of the Working Class*. 2nd ed. (kindle). London: Verso.

Kene, A. (2018). *Misty*. London: Nick Herne Books.

Kerler, D. (2017). 'Jez Butterworth's Jerusalem and Postmodern Precariousness'. Aragay, M., Middeke, M., (eds.) *Vulnerabilities, Responsibilities, Communities in 21st-Century British Drama and Theatre*. Berlin: Walter de Gruyter, pp. 63–76.

Kerrigan, S. (2022). 'Gary Owen's *Iphigenia in Splott*: The Anthropocene as Tragedy'. *Critical Stages/Scènes critiques* 26. (no pagination).

Knijff Massip, A. (2021). 'The Litigious Scene of Emancipation: A Political Analysis of Dissent in Mouthpiece (2018) by Kieran Hurley'. Translated by Charlton, N., *Estudis Escènics* 46.

Mark, L. (2024). *Theatres of Autofiction*. Cambridge: Cambridge University Press.

Mason, P. (2009). 'Butterworth's Jerusalem: The Full English'. www.bbc.co.uk/blogs/newsnight/paulmason/2009/12/butterworths_jerusalem_the_ful.html.

McEvoy, S. (2021). *Class, Culture and Tragedy in the Plays of Jez Butterworth*. Palgrave Macmillan.

McIntosh, I., Wright, S. (2019). 'Exploring What the Notion of Lived Experience Might Offer for Social Policy Analysis'. *Journal of Social Policy* 48:3, pp. 449–467. https://doi.org/10.1017/S0047279418000570.

McKinstry, L. (2021). 'How the Left Has Bullied Britain into Going for Woke'. *Daily Mail*, 8 July 2021 (updated 9 July 2021).

McKinstry, L. (2023). 'The Mail on Sunday's Woke List 2023'. *Mail on Sunday*, 30 July 2023 (updated 2 August 2023). From the male police chief who wore a menopause vest to the BBC presenter who said the Lionesses were too white | Daily Mail Online.

Monbiot, G. (2013). *Feral: Searching for Enchantment on the Frontiers of Rewilding*. London: Allan Lane.

O'Brien, D. (2020). 'Class and the Problem of Inequality in Theatre'. *Studies in Theatre and Performance* 40:3, pp. 242–250. https://doi.org/10.1080/14682761.2020.1807212.

Owen, G. (2015). *Iphigenia in Splott*. London: Oberon Modern Plays.

Paton, K. (2024). *Class and Everyday Life*. London: Routledge.

Rabey, D. I. (2015). *The Theatre and Films of Jez Butterworth*. London: Bloomsbury Methuen.

Rancière, J. (1999). *Disagreement: Politics and Philosophy*. Minneapolis: University of Minnesota Press.

Rancière, J. (2003). *The Philosopher and His Poor*. Translated by Drury, J., Oster, C., Parker, A., Durham: Duke University Press.

Ridout, N. (2013). *Passionate Amateurs: Theatre, Communism, and Love*. Ann Arbor: University of Michigan Press.

Roselt, J. (2006). 'Die Arbeit am Nicht-Perfekten'. Fischer-Lichte, E., and Gronau, B., Schouten, S., and Weiler C. (eds.), *Wege der Wahrnehmung*. Berlin: Theater der Zeit, pp. 28–38.

Runswick-Cole, K., Lawthom, R., Goodley, D. (2016). 'The Trouble with "Hard Working Families"'. *Community, Work & Family* 19:2, pp. 257–260.

Saunders, G. (2017). *Elizabethan and Jacobean Reappropriation in Contemporary British Drama: Upstart Crows*. London: Palgrave Macmillan.

Savage, M., Cunningham, N., Devine, F., et al. (2015). *Social Class in the 21st Century*. London: Pelican Books.

Savran, D. (2003). *A Queer Sort of Materialism: Recontextualizing American Theatre*. Ann Arbor: University of Michigan Press.

Scambler, G. (2018). 'Heaping Blame on Shame: "Weaponising Stigma" for Neoliberal Times'. *The Sociological Review* 66:4, pp. 766–782.

Schattschneider, E. E. (1961). *The Semi-sovereign People: A Realist's View of Democracy in America*. New York: Holt, Rinehart & Winston.

Scott, J. (1992). 'Experience'. Butler, J., and Scott, J. W. (eds.), *Feminists Theorize the Political*. London: Routledge, pp. 22–40.

Scottee (2020). *Class*. Edinburgh: Salamander Street Ltd.

Shaw, K. (2018). *Hauntology: The Presence of the Past in Twenty-First Century English Literature*. Switzerland: Palgrave Macmillan.

Skeggs, B. (2004). *Class, Self, Culture*. London: Routledge.

Skeggs, B. (2011). 'Imagining Personhood Differently: Person Value and Autonomist Working Class Value Practices'. *Sociological Review* 59:3, pp. 496–513.

Sobolewska M., Ford, R. (2020). *Brexitland*. Cambridge: Cambridge University Press.

Standing, G. (2011). *The Precariat*. London: Bloomsbury Academic.

Stanley, T. (2019). 'Britain's Cultural Elite Think Those of Us Who Voted for This Tory Landslide Are Thick Racists'. *Telegraph*, 16 December 2019. (telegraph .co.uk).

Stanley, T. (2021). 'It Shouldn't Be a Shock to the Left-Wing Media that People Vote Tory'. *Telegraph*, 10 May 2021. (telegraph.co.uk).

Telegraph Readers (2020). 'Telegraph Readers on Wealth Tax Plans: The Rich Won't Even Be Touched by It'. *Telegraph*, 9 December 2020.

Todd, S. (2014). 'The Working Classes Don't Want to Be Hard-Working Families'. *Guardian*, 10 April 2014.

Tomlin, L., McKinney, J., Bowles, J., Geary, P. (eds.) (2020). 'Artist Development: Class, Diversity and Exclusion'. *Studies in Theatre and Performance* 40:3.

Tournier-Sol, K. (2021). 'From UKIP to Brexit: The Right-Wing Populist Surge in the UK'. Tournier-Sol, K., and Gayte, M. (eds.) *The Faces of Contemporary Populism in Western Europe and the US*. Switzerland: Palgrave Macmillan, pp. 1–22.

Tyler, I. (2013). *Revolting Subjects: Social Abjection and Resistance in Neoliberal Britain*. London: Bloomsbury Academic.

Tyler, I. (2015). 'Classificatory Struggles: Class, Culture and Inequality in Neoliberal Times'. *The Sociological Review* 63:2, pp. 493–511. http://doi.org/10.1111/1467-954X.12296.

Tyler I., Slater, T. (2018). 'Rethinking the Sociology of Stigma'. *The Sociological Review* 66:4, pp. 721–743.

Valluvan, S. (2019). *The Clamour of Nationalism: Race and Nation in Twenty-First-Century Britain*. Manchester: Manchester University Press.

Virdee, S., McGeever, B. (2023). *Britain in Fragments: Why Things Are Falling Apart*. Manchester: Manchester University Press.

Waterton, C. (2003). 'Performing the Classification of Nature'. Szerszynski, B., Heim, W., Waterton, C. (eds.), *Nature Performed: Environment, Culture and Performance*. Oxford: Blackwell. pp. 111–129.

Wheeler, B. (2005). 'Who Are Britain's Hardworking Families?' BBC NEWS.

White, S. (2019). 'The Blakean Imagination and the Land in Jez Butterworth's Jerusalem'. *JCDE* 7:2: pp. 259–280. https://doi.org/10.1515/jcde-2019-0027.

Winlow, S., Hall, S. (2023). *The Death of the Left: Why We Must Begin from the Beginning Again*. Bristol: Policy Press.

Acknowledgements

I would like to thank the University of Glasgow and the Arts and Humanities Research Council (AH/W005999/1), who have supported this research and enabled open access to readers. I would also like to extend my gratitude to those who worked alongside me on my fellowship: the Advisory Board, with particular thanks to Jenny Hughes and Dave O'Brien for their invaluable support in the early stages of planning and writing this Element, and my two research assistants, Abby Jensen and Helen Shutt, who helped me with preliminary research as well as substantively managing the project events. Thanks also to Richard Gregory from Quarantine Theatre, and all those who contributed so generously to my thinking throughout the project, through symposia, workshops and the *Class Concerns* conference; and also to the IFTR Political Performances Working Group, *Resisting Theatre* conference and TaPRA's Directing and Dramaturgy Working Group, with whom early drafts of this thinking were shared. Huge thanks to my series co-editor, Trish Reid, the insightful and generous peer reviewers and all those at CUP who have supported me throughout. Finally, thanks to the many friends and colleagues who have given their time generously to the thinking-through of the project, especially Caroline Radcliffe and Sam Dobbs for their valuable feedback on early drafts.

Cambridge Elements ⁼

Theatre, Performance and the Political

Elements in the Series

A full series listing is available at: www.cambridge.org/ETPP

Printed in the United States
by Baker & Taylor Publisher Services